Preparing Children for Liturgy

A CATECHIST'S GUIDE

**by
Armandine
Kelly**

RESOURCE PUBLICATIONS, INC.
San Jose, California

Editorial director: Kenneth Guentert
Production editor: Elizabeth J. Asborno
Cover production: Terri Ysseldyke-All
Cover design: George Collopy

Reprint Department
Resource Publications, Inc.
160 E. Virginia Street, Suite 290
San Jose, CA 95112-5848

Library of Congress Cataloging in Publication Data
available.

ISBN 0-89390-155-5

5 4 3 2 1 / 93 92 19 90 89

To Mary Hicks, Carl Maugeri, Kathleen Dzura, Rev. John Cavagnaro, Barbara Dever, Joan Mullin, Rev. Michael Doyle, various worshipping communities, people with whom I've lived and/or worked, and persons who have encouraged me.

Contents

PART TWO
Celebration Preparation

PART THREE
Experience as Preparation

Acknowledgments

Thanks are due to Mary Hicks, who first asked me to write this book in magazine series form for *Modern Liturgy* in the fall of 1981. I acknowledge editorial advice from Carl Maugeri for that workshop column. Many thanks go to Kathleen Dzura, Rev. John Cavagnaro, Barbara Dever, and Joan Mullin, who critiqued this book, questioned vague passages, gave multiple suggestions for its improvement, shared liturgical experience stories, updated liturgical vocabulary and recent pastoral applications, mentioned recent resources, and encouraged me to keep going on the project. Thanks to Rev. Michael Doyle, whose networking skills found the good critiquers. The latter is the person whose blessing of the unborn, infants, and toddlers on the communion line or during the Advent blessing of pregnant mothers reminds us all that we all need to be included and acknowledged sacramentally—and when we are included from womb to tomb, our sense of God is greatly enhanced.

I am grateful to all the communities with whom I have worshiped in my life: family; friends; associates; teachers; the Sisters of St. Dominic, Newburgh, NY; the students at Providence College, Providence, RI; and workshop participants with whom I've interacted and participated.

I appreciate all who have encouraged me in my life and in my writing.

How to Read This Book

This book is intended to serve as a catechist's guidebook for preparing children for liturgical celebration. It is *not* a collection of liturgies, themes, or readings. However, it is a book about setting the stage for children to succeed at worship according to their abilities.

I have attempted to order this book in a way that encourages you to empower children to pray the liturgy by nurturing children's innate sense of life. You may, however, read it in the order that suits your needs.

The book is divided into three parts. Part One deals with sense preparation: visual, auditory, etc. Part Two provides preparation for children to understand and to pray the parts of eucharistic liturgy. Part Three underscores the power of adult example and affirmation of children during liturgical celebration. It stresses that liturgy is for life: prayer spills out into daily life and returns again. How we live life at best makes the world better or at least acknowledges the wonder of it all.

The appendices and bibliography will enable you to broaden your understanding of eucharistic liturgy so that you may empower yourself and others for quality participation in liturgical celebration and life itself.

Introduction

Tell me, I'll forget.
Show me, I may remember,
but involve me and I'll understand.
— Chinese Proverb

After watching children during eucharistic liturgy, I have recognized the need for practical guides for adults to help children cope with and experience the joy of participation in liturgy. At the heart of this concern is the belief that there is something for everyone at liturgical celebration and that everyone has something to contribute.

In the past, the Church has offered various solutions such as the "Directory of Masses with Children" and "Eucharistic Prayers for Children." Numerous writers

1

have authored dozens of "model liturgies," but the need remains for adequate involvement of a particular children's group. The present guides for children's liturgies have many good ideas but often omit children from the planning and preparation process, thus ignoring a fine opportunity for motivation and creativity.

This book will serve to present simple methods for developing and enhancing the young child's ability to celebrate eucharistic liturgy.

Some religious authorities have said children have a limited ability to appreciate prayer. Some have gone so far as to call their ability laughable, saying children are not capable of attaining a sense of God's presence and congregational, eucharistic oneness within the liturgical celebration experience. Many adults believe children are empty vessels that need to be filled—actually, children have awe, faith, sorrow, etc., that only needs to be developed. Jesus himself encouraged the little children to come to him. This book is intended to encourage all children to sense specialness and wonder, to begin knowing and experiencing liturgical celebration ritual with adult guidance.

Young children have an innate spirituality; this spirituality is often lost as they grow older. Many religious authorities have not experienced children's bedside petitionary prayer, humming happiness, and mealtime gestures of grace. They have not seen children express sorrow over broken things or dying relatives and pets. They have not witnessed children's awe in seeing a sunset or their curiosity in perceiving priest's vestments, the altar with book, bread, wine, candles, and crucifix. They have not felt children's perseverance in asking questions about the Church and eucharistic liturgy or seen children's uplifted arms while dancing in the sun or noticed children lost in thought while picking wildflowers. Why not allow children to bring all this potential to the altar of God and to celebrate all this potential as part of God's incarnation living among us? Then the child's natural spirituality may have a chance to grow and mature to the fullness of baptismal priesthood.

My proposed methods offer a way to accomplish these ends. First, I urge adults, especially parents and catechists, to use the senses to give youngsters a concrete experience of religious things, people, and expressions. Next, basic explanations, demonstrations, and a simulation of the most important parts of the eucharistic liturgy give further motivation and meaning to their liturgical expression. The final preparation involves leading children to be present physically, mentally, emotionally, and spiritually during the actual celebration of liturgy so that they realize their presence is valuable to the eucharistic gathering of God and people.

PART ONE

Sense Preparation

1

Visual: Ritual Objects

Just as Jesus used liturgical objects in worship, so do Christians. Ritual objects remain the same: baptismal water, Scripture, oil for anointing, incense, chimes, bells, the sacramentary, the vestments, the cross, and the meal of bread and wine.

Whether parenting, teaching, pastoring, ministering, catechizing, or presiding, adults help children understand liturgical objects in many ways.

Parents impart religious meanings to children by example. They answer children's questions directly and honestly. Basic answers flowing from parents' hearts and actions satisfy children.

Familiar objects reinforce spiritual meanings. Water, for instance, is necessary for daily life. Parents tell about Jesus and family members being baptized with water.

They explain how baptismal water brings new life. Water is used for blessing or sprinkling people to remind them of their baptism: dying to sin and rising with Christ to new life.

Bible stories show Jesus listening to his Father's Word. Parents and catechists guide children to listen to Scripture at home, in prayer groups, or at eucharistic liturgy.

When children ask about Jesus' meal of bread and wine, parents tell how he celebrated his Last Supper with friends as families today celebrate special events. During supper, parents explain how Jesus shared himself with bread and wine—his Body and Blood. When parents say Grace before meals, they remind children that Jesus thanked God and blessed food before he shared it. Parents tell how bread and wine, life-sustaining foods, are baked from wheat and pressed from grapes to become God's presence during liturgical celebration. Celebrating Passover or seder meals on Holy Thursdays as a family brings out the sacredness and reality of religious meals.

Parents teach the cross' meaning by gathering around it during prayer times. Parents, sensitive to children's reaction to Christ's suffering imaged on the cross, point out that Jesus rose from death to life, making the cross a life-giving sign. Using the sign of the cross prayer reinforces Trinitarian belief: Father, Son, and the mothering Holy Spirit.

I remember a confirmation class a priest gave to sixth to eighth graders and their parents. The whole lesson was on the sign of the cross. He began with the sign of the cross—not quickly as many of us do, but methodically, reverently. He explained the physical act of making a cross as a way of literally keeping in touch with the Trinity, of living in the Trinity, of doing all things in the name or persons of the Trinity, and of acting through the power of the Trinity. Then, he asked each person to make the sign of the cross slowly. Just as the mind, the heart, and the lungs work together to bring responsiveness, blood, and breath to the body, so too does the Trinity function as one God to bring life to each person and to all creation.

Teachers and catechists lead children to appreciate liturgical objects in several ways. They show labeled pictures of these ritual objects or display items on tables for each child to inspect. Opportunities for questions and answers are made. Teachers and catechists plan friendship meals with youngsters using ritual objects, substituting grape juice for wine.

Liturgical seasons are prime times for creating teachable moments. Teachers encourage older children to enact their own passion play during Lent. Doing this could bring Christ's paschal mystery right into children's hearts, where it may stay until they die. Allowing younger classes to see older classes' religious plays can often work wonders, too. Teach younger children to act out short scenes from the life of Jesus. Occasionally, entire school body passion plays are helpful but sometimes are their own passion and death when rehearsals with large numbers of children are considered. In preparing class or small-group, scripture-based plays, prayer services, paraliturgies, or liturgical celebrations, students get more involved with liturgical objects on a personal level than they do in large student body celebrations. However, both small and large group celebrations have their own value.

Ministers or priest/presiders experience many ripe situations to explain ritual objects. They meet children as individuals, within families and at parish functions, especially the sacraments and eucharistic liturgy. Priests meeting children perceptively answer their questions. They allow children to sit around or near the altar during liturgical celebration. While setting up liturgical objects for home liturgies or baptisms, they relate much to observant children. Priests can demonstrate those eucharistic liturgy parts where ritual objects are used. Priests and ministers can allow older children to role-play: using objects so youngsters experience a bit of what priests may feel while handling liturgical items: reverence, awe, and responsibility. Since children are impressionable, priests make liturgy intelligible by greeting and speaking with children in a down-to-earth manner. When priests are totally and reverently present as they pray the eucharistic liturgy with their young Christian sisters and brothers, their role in using liturgical objects takes on its richest meaning.

2

Tactile: Gesture

The kiss of peace, processions, and prayer postures have been ecclesial dimensions of eucharistic liturgy since early Christian times. Today, penitential reconciliation before offering sacrifice or gifts to God is expressed through the kiss of peace after the penitential rite or renewal of baptismal vows. Christ's presence in the people of God is manifested in liturgical processions and the whole act of worship and living. Making the sign of the cross, kneeling, sitting, standing, bowing, genuflecting, and receiving Christ's Body and Blood are visible signs of inner prayer centered around Christ's paschal mystery.

Children learn this ritual body language at an early age, but they need adults to guide them to understand its meaning. Three short stories illustrate this point.

In one church, the presider usually blesses the unborn during an Advent blessing of mothers and unborn children. He also blesses infants, toddlers, and non-receiving children, teenagers, and adults with the sign of the cross on their foreheads as they wait in the communion line with their families. One Sunday, the presider inadvertently skipped a toddler on the communion line. When the child went back to her seat, she sadly told her parents: "God didn't give me a cross." So, her parents took her to "get a cross" from the priest after liturgy was finished.

Another story is about a child who was visiting the church with her grandparents. She received the cross blessing on her forehead, and for three days she refused to let her parents wash her forehead because "God touched me there!"

A pre-school child in a different community participated in initiating the kiss of peace after a Holy Thursday foot-washing ceremony. However, not realizing that her experience was meant to be a one-time experience, the child continued to initiate the kiss of peace at the right time of liturgical celebration for the next few Sundays. She surprised all the elderly and otherwise reserved people at the end of each pew with a firm handshake!

Parents build a firm foundation for understanding the kiss of peace by being free with their affection within the home. Parents hold children's hands as protection from danger, as a sign of their love, or as a follow-up to correcting misbehavior. The outcome is new growth toward family unity. This is also true for the family of God: handshakes are signs of harmony within the Church so that all offer Christ's presence as one body with integrity. Parents can explain this to children by reading

Matthew 5:23-24: Make peace with your neighbor before you bring gifts to the altar.

At my church, the kiss of peace comes right after the renewal of baptismal promises at Eastertide or after the penitential rite outside Eastertide. The opportunity to greet people with the sign of peace at the beginning of Mass flows naturally from Matthew 5:23-24 and makes better liturgical sense as far as bodily prayer is concerned. Why? During the kiss of peace, people try to greet as many people as possible. These are short meetings requiring short attention spans. When the kiss of peace is done, the adults need a few minutes to recollect themselves before the entrance song. The children need even more time, but singing the entrance hymn centers everyone. On the other hand, during the Liturgy of the Eucharist, everyone is quietly praying with the priest. When the kiss of peace interrupts the solemnity of this prayer, everyone becomes distracted and people find it hard to get back into the quiet Lamb of God prayer.

When the kiss of peace is moved from here to the beginning of the liturgical celebration, everyone can pray the solemn Liturgy of the Eucharist, focusing on the sacramental Eucharist and the Eucharist of the people of God as one body united in a special way to Christ.

Kissing and hugging in families is often expressed to affirm love, to allay fear—even to help make a sore finger better! During eucharistic liturgy, kissing and hugging sometimes accompanies handshaking during the kiss of peace. Early Christians believed the holy kiss to be the hot-wax seal or glue on the envelope or letter of prayer or a sign of authenticity such as the "All Natural" label we see on milk and cheese in supermarkets.

Both parents and catechists show children the meaning of liturgical processions by explaining that processions are like parades. In a parade, each little group who walks is a microcosm of the community. As people see their community marching down the streets, they feel a sense of unity. They think to themselves, "This is who we are. Isn't it great!" During liturgical processions, people become Christ's quiet presence to each other, remembering his suffering, dying, and rising in today's world. They look forward to being with God eternally.

Another area of liturgical body language is prayer posture or body prayer. Parents, teachers, ministers, catechists, and presiders express inner prayer movements in various ways. On occasion, children intuitively sense when these postures are appropriate. They even model their own body prayers after those of the adults! At home or in class, it is important to sensitively get children to verbalize or act out a body prayer of how they feel during different times of the liturgical celebration. Helping children to make connections between those feeling prayers and the intentions of liturgical celebration parts is pivotal.

For instance, sitting shows receptivity to God's Word, to sung petitions, and to contributing to the offering basket. While sitting and listening, persons can remember the faith of the people in the scriptures. Then they are often aware of being a creature in God's presence.

The postures of kneeling, bowing, genuflecting, and handshaking are ways of manifesting awe, adoration, respect, thanksgiving, contrition, reconciliation, and petition. Using these postures conveys an attitude of appreciation for God's great presence in the world, in ourselves, and in others. These postures are like the Namaste bowing of the Buddhist tradition: each person folds their hands in prayer, bows to the God in each other and reverently says: "Namaste" or "I bow to God within you."

By standing, stretching the arms toward the sky, or holding the hands upward in prayer, people communicate faith, hope and love, praise, contrition and receptivity, assent, acknowledgement and a greeting (i.e., "The Lord be with you"). One presider commented that he wished the people in the congregation would lift up their arms when they answered him with "And also with you."

Standing up means many things. People stand to meet other Christians in the worshiping church and to assent to the sacramental gathering in the Great Amen. They stand to express belief in Christ's paschal mystery and to receive the Body and Blood of Christ. People stand to experience the communion of faith with the community and to sing out God's praises. Ideally, Christians stand to show their baptismal priesthood in their daily life and to convey a sense of hope for life to all they meet.

Children learn from the adults. Children may not realize all the adult meanings of the body prayer in their minds yet, but their bodies sometimes know what feels right for the circumstances. They will learn the body prayer and the inner meanings gradually over their lifetimes.

Eliciting children's feelings and showing how prayer postures express worship during prayer and eucharistic liturgy helps children bring more awareness to liturgy. Having gradually accomplished this enormous task, the children will become enriched in their newly found conscious participation in liturgy. And when they have become consciously involved, they will begin to understand and appreciate liturgical body language.

3

Kinesthetic: Liturgical Movement (Dance)

Ever since time began, human beings have expressed themselves in dance to acknowledge their awareness of God. Ancient peoples used dance to express harmony with nature. Indians adored the sun with an early morning dance. In the Judeo-Christian heritage, David danced around the Ark of the Covenant like other biblical people who danced before the Lord. Today, liturgical dancing is being revived to acknowledge the unity of body and soul before God. Children instinctively express this unity in their play and can be guided to adapt dance to sacred contexts.

To prepare children for liturgical dance, first ask children to volunteer, or choose ones naturally exuberant and graceful or confident and experienced. Explain to these children that their dancing will be a prayer for God in a special liturgy. Tell them their dance speaks for the whole congregation just as a community leader often speaks for a whole neighborhood or community. Explain that their dance is a prayer—not a performance, but a participation in liturgy. Instruct the dancers to end their dance quietly and return to sit with their group, family, or grade after the dance is completed. Lastly, arrange definite times, places, and specific music. Usually, four quarter-hour sessions are sufficient for meditative dance practices. Entrance or recessional "free form" dance preparations require only two short periods including instructions and actual practice in the liturgy place. Plan steps; however, when students are creative, knowledgeable, and expressive, incorporate their ideas while keeping the steps simple. I have successfully followed this procedure with first and second graders.

Choosing appropriate children's music for liturgical dancing is essential. Hymns that bring images to mind are ideal for liturgical dancing. Music that has a repetitive chorus helps young congregations to sing and to easily follow dancers with hand gestures. Teach all worshipers hand and head movements before liturgy time.

Several places within eucharistic liturgy lend themselves to liturgical dancing. Entrance, offertory, and recessional times are prime opportunities for processional, couple, group, and solo dancing. Movements can include skipping, hopping, sliding, walking, leaping, swinging, and swaying. Bible readings such as Hebrew Bible hero and heroine stories, canticles, psalms, New Testament parables, and the Our Father are ideal places for interpretive expression. Reflection time after Eucharist is conducive to meditative dancing with poetry and/or music.

It has been my experience that resourceful persons gifted in dance and/or sign language facilitate dance expression that is both enriching and solemnly inspiring. Children exposed to adults doing liturgical dancing again profit by example.

I remember a few instances of youngsters praying good liturgical dance. In the late 1970s, one thirteen-year-old girl danced to a modern version of the Magnificat. She danced so well, I could almost see Mary with the angel, and that whole Gospel passage came alive in an entirely new way for me.

In 1982, a parishioner's twelve-year-old daughter danced for the funeral Mass for an older nun who had become her dear friend. The youngster knew enough to choose appropriate music and to create a beautiful, tasteful dance for her departed friend. That congregation was prayerfully moved as they witnessed the girl's dance of friendship before the Lord.

Around 1987, a second-grade catechist/DRE who used six Sundays of CCD preparation for highlighting different parts of the eucharistic liturgy for her first communion students, had a pleasant surprise. Her class loved to sing Carey Landry's adaptation of the song "Peace Is Flowing Like A River" so much that some of the girls who had ballet experience made up a simple dance to that music. When it came time to have a Mass for Peace, the youngsters were ready and danced prayerfully during a meditation time. Again, people raised their hearts and minds in prayer while watching the dance.

Planning and executing liturgical dance steps for children's liturgies follow characteristics of good dance. First, varied and interesting movements—contrasting fast and slow, strong and weak, smooth and sharp—should be appropriate to rhythm and phrasing of music. Second, it is tasteful to contrast body positions such as lying, sitting, kneeling, and standing with movement, whether in place or covering ground. Individuals' visual appearance alone or in groups in relation to each other should be aesthetically appealing. Third, focus on clear and unified expressions of adoration, praise, thanksgiving, sorrow, petition, or parable consciously before God. Fourth, movement should have continuity or graceful, flowing sequence from one motion to the next. Last, prepared children should dance so that authority or holy boldness is conveyed in unity with the poetry, parable, or music.

Simple, everyday clothing that allows free movement should be worn. Token costuming for characterization should support but not distract from dance prayer. For example, a child portraying King David would wear a crown; Jesus, a purple sash across his chest; Mary, a simple blue veil; the angel, a halo on the head.

Creative use of available space for each dance will differ according to location, architecture, and flexibility of all concerned.

Above all, adults enable children to dance liturgically well when they give youngsters ample opportunities to dance before the Lord.

4

Smelling and Tasting

Sixty thousand years ago, Neanderthal people were attracted to pleasant smells and tastes. In Iraq, around the 1960s and '70s, Arlette Leroi-Gourhan excavated a Neanderthal funeral bier or stand. This bier had been covered with pine boughs, bachelor's button, hollyhock, ancient relatives of the grape hyacinth and yellow-flowering groundsel (a common European weed fed to caged birds and used in medicines). These Neanderthal people had chosen the most medicinal-tasting, sweet-smelling plants and flowers for the last rite of passage of one of their community members.

Later, the Kalihari Bushman of South Africa prized the smell and taste of golden honey. They relished their ritualized honey hunt. Each Bushman community member from oldest to youngest shared in the proceeds: the taste and smell of honey dripping from their fingers.

In early Christian times, newly baptized catechumens tasted milk and honey as part of the baptismal rite of passage—a reminder of the milk and honey of Canaan for the Israelites in the Ancient Near East. During the Middle Ages, Christians held processions and rituals where statues, flowers, and fruit were prominent features. In European countries such as Italy and Greece, this practice continues today.

Adults acknowledge children's heightened senses of smell and taste in daily life and in the liturgical environment in various ways. First, they tell children smelling and tasting stories such as the following.

Once there was an elderly lady who lived with her older brother. The brother was nearly blind, but using his sense of smell, he could tell what was going on inside and outside the house. When he smelled lemon furniture polish and Murphy's oil soap, the brother remarked how fresh and clean the house smelled. And his sister laughed, surprised that he noticed. When the brother smelled food cooking, he commented how tasty the food smelled and how he couldn't wait to taste it. And his sister chuckled, happy that he enjoyed the aroma of her cooking. When the brother smelled the air after a rain, he talked about that, too. And his sister was joyful that he was still sensitive to nature's great smells.

Thus adults can remind children that they can tell what is going on in liturgy by their using their senses of smell and taste.

Both adults and children can take an imaginary or real tour of the smells and tastes of liturgy. Go to church or class and gather the beautiful-smelling and -tasting things used during this particular liturgical season. For example, on a typical Sunday, as you enter the church or classroom, you bless yourself with holy water and listen to the bells chime. You smell the freshness of Easter water. As you pass from the church foyer into the back of the church, you see the food baskets around the gifts table for bread, wine, and Scripture. You smell the fresh flowers draping the processional cross. You smell the wicker baskets and their contents of rice, beans, noodles, cereals, cans, and other foodstuffs for the hungry. You smell the fresh-baked Eucharistic bread and the sweet, fruity wine. You smell the lit candles on the gifts table. You smell the incense: the fire and the coals. You even smell all the people: their deodorants, aftershaves, perfumes, lotions.

As you walk up to the front of the church, you smell how fresh and clean the church is for liturgy. As you near the altar, you smell the fresh altar linen and the flowers placed in strategic places: at the lectern, on the seasonal shrine altar, near the stained-glass windows, and next to the song leader's microphone.

Then you take your seat. During the entrance rite, the priest walks up the middle aisle, incensing people as he goes. As you smell it, you remember how prayer rises like incense up to God. This smell lingers for most of the Liturgy of the Word until the incense grains are burned away and the charcoal coals become cold.

During the offertory procession, you again smell the bread, wine, candles, foodstuffs, wicker baskets, and flowers.

As you pass the paschal candle decorated with fresh flowers on the communion line, you smell more flowers. As you receive eucharistic bread, you taste and smell the wheat of the Host. When you sip the eucharistic wine, you taste and smell the sweetness of grapes. You taste and see how good God is to come to us in the form of bread and wine.

Different liturgical seasons have different smells according to the flowers, fruits, and plants used to decorate the church. (See Table 4.1)

Catechists can remind children that the priest blesses all the senses during the anointing of a person before death. This is a sign of the value of the senses during life and how the person came to know God through the senses.

During a home Passover service during Holy Week, parents can use the meal to teach about taste and smell:

Table 4.1

Liturgical season	Plants, flowers, fruit candles
Advent	chrysanthemums, marigolds, Advent wreath
Christmas to Candlemas	pine, spruce trees, poinsettia, laurel, mistletoe, candles
Ordinary Time	daffodil, hyacinth
Lent	sparse arrangements or nothing
Easter	yellow/white lilies, hyacinths, geraniums, tulips
Pentecost	roses, green trees, green vines
Ordinary Time	dogwood, magnolia, daisies, poppies, lilacs, peaches, pumpkins

the taste and smell of parsley dipped in salt water, of bitter herbs with horseradish, of unleavened bread, and of roasted lamb.

Smell is a forceful sense for remembering people, places, or events. A friend told me that whenever she smells the combination of flowers and musty odors, she remembers the church she attended as a child. Then she remembers how things looked and what went on during services decades ago—all triggered by her sense of smell!

Hildegard of Bingen has good insight into the importance of smelling and tasting. In her writings and art, she pictures Adam sniffing some white flowers. She points out the fact that Adam didn't smell the flowers deeply, nor did he taste the flowers fully, nor did he touch the flowers to enjoy God's creation through his hands. For Hildegard, Adam didn't take enough pleasure from the white flowers and all of creation to maintain a life of goodness and involvement with God. She believes that his not using his senses helped lead to Adam's fall from paradise.

"To smell" is a euphemism for having an intuition; "To get a taste of..." means to experience. For the young child, the intuition or experience of worship precedes an understanding of liturgy. The child learns from others' behavior and meets new experiences with loving, joyous enthusiasm. Watch a young child crawl along the floor or walk to preschool class. The youngster smells everything, and all possible objects go into the mouth for further testing. Moreover, children experience the green palms of Palm Sunday, the blessed fruit of summer harvest, and the anointing oil of the sick or dying as part of their smelling and tasting liturgy.

Tasting is also associated with wisdom or delighting in creation. Often the Christian initiation of children is effected by the experience of the sacraments of baptism, confirmation, and first Eucharist. The children literally taste and smell how good God is as in Psalm 34:8.

When catechists and other adults encourage children to experience liturgy through smelling and tasting, the youths begin to offer their whole selves to God through these senses. And this is the whole point of preparing children for liturgy!

5

Structure: Creativity

Great celebrations arise from good planning. Liturgical celebration is no exception to this rule. One main ingredient for celebrating life's power over death is ritual. However, creativity is necessary for this celebratory proclamation. The way faith is structured and sequenced in lectionaries and sacramentaries reminds me of a recipe book. It may give steps to follow, but you won't have a cake until you bring something of yourself to the endeavor. Eucharistic rite and ritual need such creativity to infuse life into liturgical celebration. Liturgical creativity is people expressing their God-given experience in community worship and planning. When both structured ritual and creativity are present, eucharistic liturgy comes to life.

Parents, catechists, and teachers enable children to understand liturgical structure by relating events of liturgical celebration and their order to children's experience. One way is to compare liturgical celebration to special meals like Thanksgiving. Explain that when we gather for Thanksgiving dinner, we greet each other warmly and sincerely. Then, we sit, speak, and listen to older relatives relate stories from the past. In the same way, we listen to stories of God's people in readings from the Hebrew Bible and New Testament—their trials, tribulations, and struggles to know God.

It was tradition in my family to recognize my grandparents' hospitality by bringing gifts. We do this at eucharistic celebrations during the offertory procession. Next, at Thanksgiving dinner, we thanked God for the abundance of the earth and the love we received, just as we do before receiving Eucharist. When children become comfortable with experiencing meals as celebrations, it's easier for them to grasp that God is present in the form of food. We say "Amen" or "Yes" when eucharistic ministers say, "The Body and Blood of Christ," because we believe Christ is present. After sharing Thanksgiving meal, our family members gathered in the living room to sing and enjoy each other's company, just as we do throughout the liturgical celebration. Afterward, everyone leaves enriched with shared love and companionship—a true going away in peace similar to the way presiders direct us after eucharistic liturgy.

Adults can give clear explanations for what's going on at different times during liturgical celebration as youngsters ask questions. Breaking eucharistic celebration into two distinct parts helps with these explanations. Tell children that when priests recite ritual words, it begins the Liturgy of the Word; when readers proclaim Scripture, it is really God speaking to us through the Bible. The second part is the Liturgy of the Eucharist. Tell children how consecrating bread and wine helps us to remember Jesus and how he shared himself with friends at the Last Supper and now with us. As youngsters grow older, adults can expand on these explanations.

Celebrations are incomplete unless people are given chances to express their creativity. By example and encouragement, parents, catechists, and teachers help children to use creativity in church worship. This creativity can take many forms; for example, teach children to make banners, create artwork, bring flowers, and sing songs that have special meaning for them.

When adults moderately give of themselves in service and ministerial duties, they inspire youngsters to do the same, inspiring a sense of balance between their home duties and their church responsibilities. Service roles for children include breadbaking, presenting gifts, or learning hymns by heart. Tasks such as greeting people, reading, chanting prayer, and lighting incense (older children), while primarily adult activities, do reinforce for children the idea that moderate service is good. Adults distributing food to the needy, training servers, and being religious resource persons for liturgical planning and education also help to encourage the young.

While children learn by watching, it's important to remember they also learn by doing. Encourage youngsters to participate in worship and to share talents. Emphasize that children can do many things adults do at eucharistic liturgy. Although children function on simpler levels of expertise, adults can guide youngsters to appreciate liturgical celebration in a fuller way. Liturgical celebration is not a self-contained action or prayer; eucharistic liturgy ideally continues into the active/contemplative daily life of both children and adults.

6

Sounds and Silences

Although we attend eucharistic liturgy each Sunday, we may not always *hear* liturgical celebration. We know what comes next, and it is easy to mistake liturgical sounds and silences for mere repetition and thus miss its awesome mystery and beauty.

People have spoken through liturgical words and inward silences since the beginning of Christianity. The first Christians received Christ's Word in personal, family, and community ways. Inspired by history, Scripture, and Christ's paschal mystery expressed in the Eucharist, Christians, through sounds and reflective silences, remember important religious events and long for future life with God.

When parents welcome, praise, thank, forgive, express sorrow, ask for and give help to each other and their children, they lay groundwork for liturgical prayer. Also, parents can choose liturgies where everyone is welcome, especially children! Adults can sit near the altar so children can hear voices, music, bells or chimes and see everything and everyone clearly. Adult example is significant. Children imitate adults' attention to eucharistic liturgy and cooperation with ushers. Acknowledging others' presence in seating arrangements helps children realize they are part of a larger family. Bringing soft toys, crayons, and paper also helps very young children's parents to gradually introduce youngsters to liturgical celebrations. Children absorb much this way. It may seem distracting, but think back to the time when you were five or six and couldn't sit still for two minutes during eucharistic liturgy! In our church, children rarely disturb adults because children are made to feel at home. Parents who feel free to be happy, relaxed, and sensitive to others' and to children's needs in church help children realize liturgy is special.

Parents, catechists, and teachers can emphasize speaking and listening during liturgy by teaching youngsters basic prayers, responses, and acclamations, such as the Our Father, Great Amen, Alleluia, petition response, and "Holy, Holy." Adults expecting children to participate in liturgy will hear children mingling their voices with adults. Often, children learn prayers quickly when adults say them with voices that are strong and used with deep conviction or feeling. Parents and teachers can stress that the silences after Scripture readings, homily, Eucharist, and during the presider's praying are opportunities for thinking how these words apply to the particular feast or story being celebrated.

As children understand liturgical celebration parts, they can participate more. For Prayers of the Faithful, they can add prayer intentions verbally or graphically on the cantor's petition sheets. Older children can be readers, choir members, and altar servers.

By their manner of presiding, presiders can do much to elicit proper liturgical responses from children. Presiders who show happiness while celebrating liturgy put children at ease immediately. Priests who join entrance processions with feeling and who greet people with welcoming arms tell children: "Liturgy is the place to be! I need you here, too!" Proclaiming Scripture slowly, praying liturgical celebration parts distinctly, and observing silences with bodily posture tell children liturgical celebration is a holy, reverent, worthwhile action.

Children can express another silent gesture. By imitating the priest as he gestures "The Lord be with you," the children (and adults) can gesture back with their arms and voices, "And also with you." The reverent and demonstrative way presiders hold up Christ's Body and

Blood for all to say "Amen" or "So be it" evokes heartfelt responses from children about the magnificent event that is being shared.

Presiders calling people to prayer with gusto invites children to respond with gusto, too. Hopefully, presiders celebrate the entire eucharistic liturgy with gusto! Acknowledging children by name as they receive Eucharist will help children realize that Christ is calling them to respond "Amen" and then continue to express Eucharist to others through daily Christian actions. Acknowledging children and adults who haven't received first communion yet with a blessing on the forehead or a laying of hands on the shoulders or head includes the entire worshiping community sacramentally in the eucharistic liturgy.

When adults are attuned to liturgy's sounds and silences, their example and teaching enables children to develop these prayer rhythms. Then, liturgy is faithfully communicated.

7

Auditory: Music

Prehistoric peoples used rhythm and sound to express prayerful feelings. They imitated flowing streams, wind, rain, thunder, singing birds, and other animal sounds. As language developed, human beings combined chanted poetry with music. Later, people sang Psalms, Gregorian chants, and hymns while playing instruments. Now people express prayerful feelings by using classical, traditional, and contemporary sacred music. Today's children chant as they jump rope, sing hand-clapping games, and play ring-around-the-rosey. With adult direction, children can apply their musical experience to sacred music.

When helping children with liturgical music, musicians, catechists, and teachers should start where all concerned can function musically. Choose music from albums such as Carey Landry's *Color the World,* or compose simple, melodic music and words reflecting Scripture, prayer, or religious themes. Encourage children to make up psalm versions and compose songs for these. Write down their melodies, then use the best ones.

Teach songs by reviewing familiar ones first. Make a list of these. Learn new songs yourself. Then present new lyrics to the children. Sing the songs twice, inviting children to hum along first and then to sing.

Have a spirit or unity song that you can use to gather, to process, to parade, or to celebrate any occasion. One school uses "To Be Alive" by Ray Repp, which brings the children together in joy. Choose a song that the youngsters love to sing—something that celebrates their lives as children, as friends, as members of families.

As each new liturgical season approaches, teach two or three songs for that season. Sing these songs each week for prayer, paraliturgies, prayer services, and eucharistic liturgy. By the middle of the liturgical season, the children will know the songs by heart. For example, during Lent, one school's focus song was "I Have Decided to Follow Jesus." As reinforcement to the song, the younger grades used hand motions with the song while the upper grades discussed in religion class their faith commitment.

Find or make up a sung response for the Prayer of the Faithful. One group sings "Lord, we ask you, hear our prayer." Do this and you may find that the children's attention to the petitions is more focused as they wait to sing their response to each petition.

Show the children what to do. Will they echo after you or just sing choruses? Should they listen to meditative song or sing verses? Are children to sing response phrases several times? Will they process or hold candles as they sing? Should youngsters sing psalm responses at beginning and end only or will they sing between verses? Do they sing with or without accompaniment? Do choir members or song leaders sing meditative songs? Can instruments or choir introduce a piece to be sung by all? Involve children in planning answers to these questions.

Scripture readings such as Mary's Magnificat, poems, or canticles from the Hebrew Bible or New Testament can be sung within the greater context of the scripture passage, which is largely read by the priest or first or second reader. For this, the singer or singers should be of the highest quality. Also, these types of readings might appear only once or twice a year. Youngsters sing best when they know everything by heart. Using familiar songs with one or two new pieces helps participation. Group singing should prevail, not choirs or solos, because liturgy is everyone's prayer, not an elite performance. Choirs and solos, sung or instrumental, are strictly for supportive meditative use.

Exposing children to good contemporary, traditional, and sacred classical music enriches their response to Word and Eucharist. Leave a record or tape player with records and cassettes for children to use during their free time at church, at school, in the parish resource room, and at home.

Introduce the children to good music. Choose songs with concrete inspiring poetic imagery. Let messages convey that God is near but also mysterious. Utilize music that has appropriate rhythm, engaging melody, and adequate harmony. Music should convey factual meaning with ease. Words and music must inspire holy feelings as well as reflect real life.

You might include the following requirements on your checklist for choosing music:

1. Prayerful — to proclaim and celebrate God's Word

2. Solemn — to educate and inspire religious feeling

3. Unifying — to encourage commitment to God and to each other

Adults should pick lyrics and music that express particular liturgical moments. For example, the Gospel Alleluias are strong, rousing hoorays, whereas psalm responses are quiet, meditative pieces.

When choosing to sing only some liturgical celebration parts, the Gospel Alleluias; Holy, Holy; and Great Amen have first preference. Afterward, it's good to sing psalms, the Memorial Acclamation, and communion hymn. For Sunday celebrations, entrance and closing hymns, the Lord's Prayer, peace-giving music (during the sign of peace) and Lamb of God are important to sing with the first-preference pieces cited above. Additional options include the prayer of the faithful, presentation of gifts, preface, fraction (of the Host), and hymn of thanksgiving. Music should complement existing quiet times.

Practiced musicians, whether children or adults, should accompany singing as song leaders. Young children can use rhythm instruments such as clapping sticks, small hand drums, triangles, small bells, etc.

Instrumental tone quality should fit the mood of particular eucharistic liturgy portions. Organs accompany entrance hymns while autoharps accompany psalms. Pianos aid meditative and transitional spots, whereas the guitar or double bass may accompany voices, another instrument, or just play a solo meditation piece.

Many possibilities exist for tasteful liturgical music with children. Adults can provide these opportunities, thus enriching children's participation and enjoyment of the eucharistic liturgy.

8

Atmosphere

Through the ages, people have worshiped God within various settings and locations. Primitive people gathered in circles outdoors under sun, moon, and stars. They gathered at mountains, volcano sites, trees, caves, burial mounds, fires, and canyons. Although sites differed, each sacred place contained something that focused community attention on God.

Later, as civilization brought worship indoors, people brought nature, sacrificial meals, religious symbols, water, incense, and images inside. They painted cave and building walls, stained glass, and sculpted statues to enhance community worship. They created environments that expressed who they were as a prayerful community.

Today, after centuries of following traditions popular in the Middle Ages, people are still creating worship environments that reflect their society.

Adults can encourage youngsters to create their own worship environments to deepen their liturgical celebration experience outside the actual liturgy space, the church. First, get children to think about alternative places for liturgy: a chapel, a classroom, a meeting room, etc. Ask them what places they would like to dedicate to God. Some guidelines are helpful. Is the desired place available for use during the time needed? Are accommodations adequate for group size and liturgical actions? Look for sufficient heat, light and ventilation. Are acoustics good? Will liturgy take place without interruption? Young worshipers should be near the table, reading place, and cross. Having youngsters think about these things will help them appreciate the church atmosphere even more.

For paraliturgies and prayer services, plan decorations based on yearly and liturgical seasons or on children's saint or hero stories, favorite games, or a recent event such as birthdays or funerals. Employ symbols such as family photos, baseball caps, or fairy tale characters; place these on a special table or cloth in the room. Ask the children for ideas for decorations. One teacher's second-grade students came up with the idea of making an archway of kites for the Holy Spirit's wind during Pentecost. Another group made a gigantic creation story banner and cut it into large jigsaw puzzle pieces. Then the students hung the jigsaw pieces on separate banner poles. At the end of the liturgy, the students held all the pieces of the jigsaw banner together to make a complete picture of the creation story. It was quite an eye opener!

A good way to assure variety in environments is to plan the year's celebrations according to the liturgical seasons, their special colors, and general focus. (See Table 8.1.)

In the church setting, adults can enable children to create an environment focusing on liturgy and unity. Guide children to use liturgically colored vestments, altar cloths, garlanded crosses, and flowers. Make sure the chosen things blend well with traditionally accepted church decorations.

Introduce the children to the idea of a shrine altar for special liturgical season decorations. What is a shrine altar? The shrine altar is a Russian and Greek Orthodox tradition many centuries old. In Russia, Orthodox Christian couples whose children were grown up were encouraged to travel to hermitages and live as praying hermits for extended periods of time. They also extended hospitality to travelers. To let a visitor know that the traveler was entering a hermitage house, the door was often painted light blue and the foyer inside had a

Table 8.1

Liturgical season	Color(s)	Purpose
Advent	purple, pink	waiting for the Lord
Christmas to Candlemas	white	celebrating Incarnation
Ordinary Time	green	celebrating Christ's mission
Lent	purple	atoning for sin, practicing social justice
Easter	yellow, white	realizing the Resurrection
Pentecost through Ordinary Time	red, green	appreciating the Holy Spirit's role in our lives

special icon with a lit candle beside it. The visitor then knew to keep a hushed voice, accept hospitality, and respect the solitude of those within the hermitage. The place of the icon was called a shrine altar. Shrine altars were later adopted by families and communities.

Many old churches still have extra altars dating back to the time when priests said private masses in Latin. Today, one of these extra altars can be transformed into a shrine altar for icons, remembrances of the particular liturgical season or feast, and reminders to pray for the dead on November 2. Our church's shrine altar is a constant reminder of where we are in the church year and what feast we are celebrating on a particular Sunday. It is set up on such a way that it enhances but does not detract from the focus of the eucharistic altar.

Making a shrine altar is easy. At home, parents can make a shrine altar from a small table, putting on it the Bible, a book of icons, a candle or oil lamp, and a decorative cloth. In class, catechists and teachers can make a similar shrine altar with their students in a classroom. DREs and CCD teachers can make shrine altars in chapels and general purpose rooms.

In the church setting, direct children to create a shrine altar at a side altar or table. Get the permission of the pastor first, though; he may be able to help you decide the best place for it. Allow children to decorate the shrine altar with icons or children's symbolic religious pictures of heroes, heroines, saints, relatives, small banners of themselves and who they are, baskets of nature things for the season, or their drawings and religion projects. These will accentuate children's identity as a faith community. Children can sense God's care for them when they put part of themselves on a shrine altar. Use decorations on a one-time basis so they don't fade into the woodwork after a while (or preempt the adult's use of the shrine altar).

For weekdays and designated children's Sundays (Respect Life Sunday, St. Francis, Carnivale Sunday), children can decorate the church's patron saint statues with flowers for the name day liturgies. During Lent, light stations of the cross with lamps or candles. Spotlight stained-glass windows and wall or ceiling murals if they depict the day's scriptural readings. Children can place decorated baskets holding fresh bread and tasteful decanters containing chilled wine on an offertory table with lectionary, candles, flowers, and cross. Taking time to consider this arrangement can lead children to see Word and Eucharist as liturgy's main focus. Once older children get over the strangeness of incense, guide them to use it—very carefully! This will give them a sense of prayer, filling the world and drawing all people to God. The baptismal font can be decorated to celebrate children's baptismal days by hanging photos or baptismal certificates around it—signs of being part of Christian community.

Finally, a brief slide show or film showing the children interacting as a community further solidifies their identity in worship. Use filmstrips, slides, films, or film videos with religious, instrumental music or liturgical songs the children enjoy. One good technique is to get the older children to make the slide shows. Psalms or readings are also appropriate to compliment pictures. The more children invest in liturgy, the more they'll derive from being together and sharing Christian ministry with each other.

PART TWO

Celebration Preparation

9

Gathering

Since time began, people have come together to worship God. Ways they gathered reflected how they cared for each other's needs and shared basic concerns. Preparing themselves for common prayer, people sensed a readiness for oneness. They remembered seasons and feasts; people brought their handiwork, positioned worship symbols and prayed for each other. Today's parish liturgy gatherings continue with these historic patterns.

Adults guide children to gather for eucharistic liturgy. Making opportunities for children to be part of family, small group, or class liturgies encourages young children to gather with individuals they know. This context allows for relaxed settings not often possible in whole school liturgies.

Parents model gathering behavior for Sunday liturgy. Even though they may have rushed to get to church on time, parents get into the worship spirit by greeting people at the door, asking for prayers to be put on the petition sheet, getting a song sheet, and putting food in baskets for the poor. As they wait for Mass to begin, parents can explain the feast or Scripture readings for the day. In pointing out religious signs around them, parents satisfy children's religious curiosities and understandings. By their example, parents help children experience quiet and settling down. Parents can also direct children's attention to the shrine altar, if the church has one. This will focus everyone's attention on the feast of the day or the liturgical season. Children are sensitive to adult behavior and will copy it.

Teachers and catechists continue parents' work as they gather children in small groups for liturgy. Fostering positive experiences of small group prayer almost ensures enduring interest in worship for children. Youngsters in class settings can express themselves in prayer quietly and without the pressures of being compared with older students. This way, children develop their identity as the Body of Christ—a little Church. Small children, like Zaccheus, want to know Jesus better but they can't see over taller people's heads. They need to climb trees and catch Jesus' attention. Just as Zaccheus went out an a limb and received Jesus as a supper guest, so, too, small children can experience this by gathering in little circles.

Through prayer activities and role playing, teachers and catechists emphasize with children how people gather. With guidance, students can share how they meet Christ in others by doing little things: making other students feel at home in prayer circles, making room for slow movers or shy youngsters. Students can remember and experience Christ's presence by listening attentively to each other's prayer intentions. Youngsters can be directed to share briefly what they think and feel about their problems and how Christians try to solve them. Teachers and catechists remind students that gathering for worship with peers is an extension of what they experience with families.

Mystery is part of gathering. Students need to realize the seriousness and awe of celebrating. They need to know it's connected to their whole lifetime of dying and rising in Christ.

By tailoring gathering time before liturgical celebration to fit children's attention spans, teachers and catechists relieve students who may want to behave but are not always able to do so.

When gathering children for eucharistic liturgy, everyone "gets it together" by bringing their whole selves to share prayers, concerns, material things, life symbols, and quiet presence. Adults teach children to be signs of Christ by acknowledging other's presence. Simple considerations such as taking seats quietly, respecting neighbors' stillness, developing capacities for quiet time, and remembering reasons for gathering will aide children to be hospitable and prayerful and to sense community ties. Also, their responses during liturgical celebration will soon reflect spontaneity, naturalness, and sincerity.

10

Reconciliation and Renewal

For many years, people of various cultures have had religious reconciliation ceremonies. For over a thousand years, Jewish people participated in penitential rituals before regular synagogue services. For hundreds of years, Native Americans smoked and passed one sacred pipe among a circle of equals to show a settling of differences and a unity with the Great Spirit. In early Christian times, the Didache recorded that worshipers should break bread and give thanks only after confessing their sins. In today's Church, penitence during introductory Mass rites allows people to renew relationships with God and others as advised in Matthew 5:23-24: Make peace with your neighbor before bringing gifts to the altar.

Adults help youngsters understand liturgy's penitential rite in several ways. Basically, parents explain that after people wrong another person, they are sad that the other person was hurt. After thinking about it, they finally say to the hurt person that they are sorry, and they ask forgiveness. The hurt person then forgives them and the friendship is renewed. Often, people may become better friends than before because each has shown that they value their relationship. One family I know practices forgiveness in their daily lives. They talk over the hurts of the day, forgive each other, and then sing Carey Landry's song, "Peacetime," as a healing closure for the day.

Parents also aid children's understanding of penitence by illustrating with a story. Using a familiar situation such as a birthday party, the story might go something like this: Sue's good friend, Bill, invites her to his birthday party. A few days before, while playing a game, a dispute arises. Both are angry and say the other is wrong. After thinking things over, Sue realizes she is wrong and doesn't feel like going to Bill's party. Her mother helps her buy a gift, but Sue's heart isn't in a party mood. Birthday party time comes and Sue reluctantly goes, carrying her present. Arriving at Bill's house, she finds time to tell Bill she's sorry. He forgives her.

Later, Sue gives her gift to Bill and it becomes a token of their renewed friendship.

Teachers and catechists, building upon parental explanations, show children four parts of penitential rites. First, priests invite all worshipers to remember any wrongdoing they've committed against God or each other. Second, everyone is briefly silent so each person can examine his/her recent behavior. Third, people admit their guilt by praying together the Confiteor ("I confess..."), asking the saints to help us. Other penitential prayers such as penitential psalm verses or a "Lord have mercy" litany may be used in place of the Confiteor. Another way to recognize sinfulness is to renew baptismal promises and pray during a cleansing water sprinkling ceremony called "Asperges me" ("Sprinkle me"). Last, presiders request forgiveness and God's mercy upon all present.

Parents, teachers, catechists, and priests remind children that kneeling down outside of Eastertide helps us to express sorrow for wrongdoing, whereas standing helps us to renew our baptismal vows during the Easter season.

Acknowledging sinfulness before God prepares everyone to listen to God's Word better and to share in Eucharist with ready hearts. Adults help children by pointing out hurtful behavior and gently guiding children to examine their feelings. They encourage youngsters to heal broken relationships through renewed Christian commitment, often shown in the kiss of peace. (See chapter 2 for more in-depth discussion about the kiss of peace.) The whole penitential rite prepares children to be purposefully and personally present at liturgy.

Above all, adults enable children to express their offenses against God and faults against others so that they, as God's people, will know their limitations better, name themselves as Christians, and rejoice in renewing their relationships as God's children and sisters and brothers of each other: the Gospel "neighbor."

11

Entrance

Since the fifth century, eucharistic liturgy has begun with introductory ceremonies now called the entrance rite. This rite alerts church community to begin liturgy as one body. It signifies the initial group participation in liturgical celebration after people have been individually greeted and welcomed in church that day.

Adults teach children the two important parts of the entrance rite: the entrance song and opening prayer or Collect. An entrance song is a community prayer uniting all as the Body of Christ. As everyone listens, the presider uses the opening prayer to collect private prayer, offers it to God, and states liturgical season's or feast's message from the sacramentary or book of liturgical prayers.

Teach children entrance rite sections in proper sequence. First, a leader invites all to sing the beginning hymn as a simple procession begins, usually at the back of church. People processing are:

1. minister carrying a cross

2. reader lifting up lectionary or book of Bible readings

3. servers bearing candles

4. priest/presider using incense or sprinkling people with holy water.

Speaking about incensing and sprinkling, the priest in our parish feels that the holiest walk he takes all week is the one coming down the aisle during the entrance song. As he bows to people while incensing and sprinkling them, he feels aware that he is incensing or sprinkling God within the people. It is a powerful experience of prayer for him.

The following sequence illustrates how a teacher or parent can explain the entrance rite. After the people in the procession seat themselves and singing concludes, the presider greets the congregation briefly, enthusiastically, and distinctly. Then, most parishes take part in a penitential rite or renewal of baptismal promises with the "Lord Have Mercy." The Gloria, when included in the rite, takes place before the opening prayer and ideally should be sung. Then the priest says, "Let us pray," pauses briefly to collect the unspoken prayers of the people, and prays the opening prayer from the sacramentary. When used properly (if at all!), the pause can be powerful! Now the presider utilizes this important opening prayer to gather congregational prayer and then continues the seasonal or festal theme. The entrance rite ends as the server returns the sacramentary to its place.

As youngsters come to understand the Entrance Rite sections, teachers, parents, catechists, and priests can demonstrate ways to participate in the rite. Adults or teenagers can do this effectively by acting out a sample entrance rite for children. After observing the rite closely, have all the children act out rite parts as though they were at liturgy. Remind children to respond to the presider in full voice when they say "Amen" or "And also with you." Emphatic speaking shows they understand and agree with what's being said. Train youngsters to listen to the entrance song's message as they stand and heartily sing. This opening hymn usually introduces a theme for the liturgical season or feast being celebrated. St. Basil said singing makes praying easier; so, when preparing to receive both Word and Eucharist, a rousing hymn helps people to pray in heart and mind. Another good idea is to rehearse a procession. Let them feel how movement down a central aisle toward the altar enables them to pay closer attention to liturgy. Seeing objects carried in procession reminds everyone of what's being done:

1. The cross gives hope in Christ's power over death while the lectionary, God's Word, manifests the historical Presence.

2. Candles light a path as the presider incenses all with the odor of prayer or sprinkles holy water on people reminding them of baptism.

Finally, practice the Collect, or opening prayer. Direct one youngster to play the presider's role by enunciating, "Let us pray" and briefly pausing. During the pause, instruct everyone to say a brief, silent prayer to God. After the pause, have the student/presider symbolically collect the private prayers and present them to God by praying a sample opening prayer from the sacramentary.

By going through all these steps and by being observant during liturgical celebration, children will gradually become aware and participate more fully during the Entrance Rite. They will understand it because adults allow them to fully experience it.

12

The Word

Our present structure of the Liturgy of the Word dates back to 44 A.D. when the Jewish Christians began worshiping apart from synagogue services. In the fourth century, trained lectors read three predetermined Scripture readings after a presider's greeting. Then people responded in song, listened to homilies, and held common prayer.

Parents, teachers, catechists, and priests can stress to children that the Liturgy of the Word's heart is found in the following three actions:

1. readers proclaiming the Word

2. people's listening and responding

3. the presider giving the homily

God is present with people through the spoken Word. As people reflect on Scripture's meaning, they respond to it in silence, song, and acclamation. Then the homilist applies God's Word to today's Christian living.

Adults can make main events of the Liturgy of the Word come alive for children in the following way. Explain that the first lector tells a Hebrew Bible story. Stress that these stories were written before Christ was born. People then silently reflect on this reading and respond by singing a psalm antiphon and listening to a psalm or holy poem as it is sung or read. Teaching children how to reflect on readings is difficult but important. One technique is to get children to use their imagination. Tell the children to visualize a nature setting and use their five senses to get a picture or sense of wonder about what God has created. Some readers may give children a few extra moments to reflect on readings. An excellent resource for further ideas is Theresa Scheihing Cutler's Credence Cassette tapes and her meditation book. She deals specifically with techniques for helping children to pray.

Next, a second minister delivers a New Testament reading from the apostolic letters. After people sing the Gospel acclamation or "Alleluia," a third reader, usually the presider, proclaims the Gospel or Good News, written by Matthew, Mark, Luke, and John. Then, the homilist makes the Word relevant and hope-inspiring for modern church people. Again, all reflect for some time. The Word reminds all of their religious roots—the Judeo-Christian stories of our faith. After silence, people stand to recite the Creed, the summary of Catholic beliefs. If parents, teachers, catechists, and priests teach one main lesson about the Liturgy of the Word, it should be this: God's message is that God has been present with people in the past, God is present with people now, and God wants all people to be present with God forever. God says this as Father, Son, and the mothering Holy Spirit, the Trinity.

A prayer service would be an ideal situation for children to know more about the Liturgy of the Word. At home or in school, adults can use the upcoming Sunday readings to prepare children for a brief celebration at the end of the week. A few days before the service, choose good readers from family or class as lectors for readings and practice reading slowly and distinctly with them. Get volunteer singers who, with adult supervision, will prepare the responsorial psalm and Gospel acclamation. Prepare singers by using a tape, record, or musical instrument during their practice time. Prepare readers by using a microphone. Instruct them to read slowly. All too often, academically good readers read so quickly that the congregation misses the whole story! Read over each Bible reading with family or class and summarize the main ideas after each reading. If readings are too long for children, have several readers read parts of the passage. Be patient with children's responses. Guide them to apply the message to their own lives in some way. Go over formal responses to readings so youngsters respond wholeheartedly with "Thanks be to God" and "Praise be to you, Lord Jesus Christ." Teach children to sing the psalm antiphon and Gospel acclamation with the song leader. Sing them both whenever there is time.

Plan a specific time and place for the prayer service. Teach all the children how to use a microphone properly, and practice using it on a regular basis. Practicing includes raising and lowering a stationary microphone stand. An adult can prepare a short homily that will relate the readings to children's experiences. Now you're ready.

Follow the order for the Liturgy of the Word. Leave the Bible or lectionary with readings clearly marked at a lectern or table. Sit for the first two readings; stand for the Gospel acclamation and Gospel; sit for the homily. When all is done, praise the children for their hard work. You might give them a certificate as a concrete reminder they can hang on their refrigerator at home. Or give each a bookmark or index card with a phrase of Scripture that summarizes one of the readings. These cards can be embellished with simple stickers or stick drawings. One teacher put the saying: "Don't be afraid. I am with you" and on a blue card with a small design of a boat cut from wrapping paper. The story had been about Jesus being in the boat during the storm and how he calmed everything and everybody.

With a little luck, children will remember the experience of the Liturgy of the Word and carry over what they have learned to Sunday liturgy.

13

The Word with Children

The children's Liturgy of the Word within the context of adult liturgy is a phenomenon of the late 1980s. In pre-Vatican times, before 1963, many parochial elementary schools worshiped as student bodies on Sundays, holy days, etc., while adults attended other masses. Both children and adults celebrated Mass the same way, and both masses were in Latin. In the post-Vatican period, during and after 1963, children and adults participated in liturgical celebrations in English, often as distinct worship groups with music and homilies tailored for congregational age and ability. In 1987, some churches began to integrate the needs of both grownups and youngsters within the adult eucharistic liturgy with one change. The change was an adult Liturgy of the

Word in church and a children's Liturgy of the Word in a chapel, classroom, or other room. The two occurred simultaneously within one liturgical context of eucharistic liturgy.

The advantages of doing eucharistic liturgy in this new way are numerous. First, families come and go to church together on Sundays. Second, very young children listen to God's Word in a small group setting, knowing that they'll be back with their families in twenty to thirty minutes. Third, youngsters take turns preparing and reading Bible passages. Fourth, children listen to a homily they can understand. Fifth, children sing hymns and pray prayers meaningful to children.

How does this children's Liturgy of the Word fit into Sunday liturgical celebration? Families sit together for the beginning of liturgy. After the presider finishes the Collect prayer and sits down, the children's minister of the Word goes to the middle aisle in front of the church and raises up the lectionary. Chimes ring once. Soft music plays. Next, children line up and follow their minister of the Word to another room; some parents and adults go to help the minister. Then, both children and adults begin the Liturgy of the Word in different places.

The children's minister leads the children's Liturgy of the Word. That person introduces the name and meaning of the Sunday feast and applies this to the children's life experience. Two children or adults read the first two Scripture passages. For the responsorial psalm, all children sing a psalm-based hymn from an album such as *Psalms Alive* by the Maranatha! Singers ("The Lord Is My Shepherd," "This Is the Day That the Lord Has Made"). Next, the minister reads the Gospel and gives a homily relating the day' scriptures to the children's daily life. Then, the minister gives a ritual message of summary of the Word to each individual child. For example, "Today, Jesus says to you, N., be like the seed that fell on good ground." Finally, the minister gives each child an index card, a bookmark, or a pen with the message and symbol for the day imprinted on it. The symbol compliments the message: a popcorn seed scotch-taped to the card compliments the above cited message. Then, all quietly return to church to sit with their families—in time for the offertory procession and the litany prayers of the faithful.

Some churches keep the children longer and do a project using charts, questions boxes, dialogue readings, pantomime game techniques, or audio-visuals with a short homily or in place of a homily. In other churches, the children's minister of the Word walks up the aisle with the adult's minister of the Word. Sometimes, before the children depart from church, the presider blesses the children's minister and aide with these words: "Receive the Word of God and proclaim it to our children as we shall have it proclaimed to us, in the name of the Father..." One church requires the minister to end the children's Liturgy of the Word with the Creed, a prayer of the faithful, a song, or another prayer. Most churches have a messenger to inform the children's minister that the adult homily is almost finished.

Other details in the children's Liturgy of the Word include setting up beforehand a room, prayer rug, or lectern with candle and other needed materials. Someone also has to clean up afterward. Another concern is scheduling people for two or three consecutive sessions, so that children and adults get used to each other and sense together a continuity of the liturgical season, scripture readings, style expectations, and reinforcements of songs, prayers, etc. Most churches have a general outline for children's ministers of the Word to follow. Also, many churches have source books for children's ministers to borrow.

The aim of the children's Liturgy of the Word is to expose the children to the adult structure and content in terms of the child's mind or ability to understand. Most churches achieve this solemnity with simple but basic pastoral theology and application. Please don't use cutesy ideas, songs, and projects that talk down to children and allow them to miss the connection with prayer and Scripture. The children need to come away with a sense of rite and ritual that will ready them for the adult Liturgy of the Word upon reaching junior high and beyond.

Now that the phenomenon is explained, how do you prepare children to participate in the children's Liturgy of the Word? (Preparation is the key word in this book, after all!) The answer is that you prepare children in the same way you prepared them for the Word in an entire children's liturgy. (See the previous chapter for details.)

How will the children respond to the children's Liturgy of the Word? In my church, the response has been very positive. I spoke with some second through fourth graders and these were some of their responses:

"I get to read the Bible!"

"I like praying."

"I like helping the person [minister]"

"I like going [to the Liturgy of the Word]."

"I like passing out stuff."

"I like the songs about the Lord!"

Before I end this chapter, I'd like to recount what a Pennsylvania community was doing before the children's Liturgy of the Word became implemented in most of the Delaware Valley. The community had a program for children from birth to age twelve and called it a Ministry of Care. Their age groupings and activities are noteworthy. From birth to age two-and-a-half, adults played religious and classical religious music (i.e., "Ave Maria") and told simple Bible stories. For ages two-and-a-half to four, the minister told Bible stories, gave a simple snack, had a short activity related to the stories, and sang songs with them. Children ages five through eight had the Liturgy of the Word with the adults doing the readings and structuring the activities within a short homily and religious songs or psalms. Children ages nine to twelve helped to plan activities and songs, and practiced the readings for the Liturgy of the Word. After their confirmation, the young people were introduced to the complete adult liturgy.

14

Transition from Word to Eucharist

Ever since 150 A.D., early Christians have chanted together for themselves and for the world petitions during liturgical celebrations. Then, priests received people's gifts of money and food and set aside bread and wine for Eucharist. These practices continue in today's liturgy.

Adults can explain to children that two actions connect Liturgy of the Word to Liturgy of the Eucharist: the prayer of the faithful and the preparation of gifts. The prayer of the faithful is a universal litany of prayer for both the local congregation and the world. We chant or recite the litany or list of prayers after the homily. This marks the end of the Liturgy of the Word. As food, money, bread, and wine are brought up, a presider receives these gifts, arranges bread and wine in suitable containers, and prays over them. This prepares the altar for Liturgy of the Eucharist.

Parents, teachers, catechists, and priests define the prayer of the faithful to youngsters by explaining that it is a petition list or litany of things we ask God for in prayer. Through this ancient prayer, people ask God to bless everyone—somewhat like the way children do at bedtime prayers. A basic litany would read as follows:

1. For the salvation of the world and for civil and world authorities...

2. For church needs and leaders...

3. For all here present and benefactors...

4. For oppressed people...

5. For the sick...

6. For the dead...

A litany reader reads or chants these and adds "Let us pray to the Lord" after each petition. The community answers by saying or chanting "Lord have mercy" or similar response. The litany ends with its own concluding prayer.

Instruct children that there are several steps after the litany in preparation of the gifts. First, ushers collect money from worshipers. Next, appointed people take up bread, wine, food, and money to the priest. Gradually, priest and servers set the table for Eucharist with napkin, plate of bread, chalice and carafe of wine, and a small sacramentary. The priest prays quietly. then invites people to pray and respond. Lastly, people stand as the presider prays the prayer over the gifts. Everything is now ready for Eucharist to begin.

Familiarize children with the universal litany and gift preparation by acting out parts with them. Guide students to make up their own list of petitions covering the areas already mentioned. Also, encourage them to name specific people appropriate to each category. Next, explain that petitions are usually sung or recited; teach one good singer (or speaker) from family or class to chant the litany. Prepare everyone to answer each petition with a sung or recited "Lord have mercy." Direct the singer to conclude the litany with a prepared prayer to which all respond, "To You, O Lord" (sung or recited).

Make the preparation of gifts meaningful to students by assigning roles of ushers, gifts carriers, congregation, and presider to specific group members. Guide each person to perform specific jobs and to verbalize reasons for each action. For example, ushers with baskets could say, "Poor people need you to share time, talents, and money with them." Persons bringing up food can say, "This food goes to the hungry people in our neighborhood." Then, bread and wine carriers may say, "These will be shared by all. We're remembering what Jesus did at the Last Supper." "Priest" and "servers" now set the table and inform everyone, "We're almost ready." End the whole tableau by having the "presider" pray the prayer over the gifts.

Making the transition from Liturgy of the Word to Liturgy of the Eucharist concrete for children enables them to understand and enjoy this part of the eucharistic liturgy.

15

The Eucharist

During the Last Supper, Jesus gave thanks to the Father over bread and wine with his friends. Then, he proclaimed the bread and wine to be his Body and Blood, broken and poured out to save all people. Jesus asked his disciples to remember him whenever they had a similar sacred meal.

Explain the Liturgy of the Eucharist as having two major parts: the eucharistic prayer and communion rite. During the eucharistic prayer, people give thanks for God's caring actions; they bless bread and wine in remembrance of Jesus' suffering, death and resurrection. In the communion rite, people break bread, pour wine, and share Jesus' Body and Blood in union with God and each other.

Parents, teachers, catechists, and priests can instruct youngsters on how people participate in the Liturgy of the Eucharist. People actively agree with what the celebrant prays in the thanksgiving prayer by responding or singing agreements called acclamations. The three most important acclamations (usually sung) are Holy, Holy; Proclamation of Faith; and Great Amen. Recited acclamations include "And also with you," "We lift them up to the Lord," and "It is right to give Him thanks and praise." Responses from eucharistic prayers for children 1, 2, and 3 can also be included and practiced. For the communion rite, adults prepare children for the Our Father, sign of peace, Lamb of God, communion reception ("Amen," procession, meditation pause or song) and concluding prayer.

One good way to involve the children in the Liturgy of the Eucharist is to have a family or class thanksgiving meal. Plan and practice all details of the eucharistic prayer and communion rite a week or two in advance. Also, familiarize youngsters with appropriate Communion songs. Choose alert singers to lead acclamations and five (or less) good children or adult readers to pray presider's parts in the eucharistic prayer (preface, etc.). Then, train servers to assist when needed. Get a student leader or adult as presider for the communion rite and prepare it. On the appointed day, set a table for your thanksgiving meal, but substitute grape juice for wine. Bake your own unleavened bread. Have necessary dishes ready. Just before you begin, remind children to bring a sense of wonder, thanks, and praise to glorify God. Finally, in memory of Jesus, bless, break, eat, and drink. It will be a memorable event.

16

Dismissal and Recession

In the early days of the Church, priests usually sent liturgical celebration participants right home after communion with Eucharist for sick or absent family members. Later in history, when the Eucharist became more adored from afar than shared, people lacked a sense of mission to concretely share the eucharistic bread with others outside eucharistic liturgy. And so, the dismissal rite and recessional music became final parts of liturgical celebration, giving liturgy a good group sense of closure or ending.

Today, explain to children that the dismissal rite and recessional music bring an end to modern liturgical celebration. The dismissal rite briefly and directly tells people Mass is over. Recessional music concludes the celebration aspect of liturgy.

Parents, teachers, catechists, and priests can inform children about the dismissal rite procedure in the following way. First, priests or lectors make brief community announcements regarding baptisms, sicknesses, deaths, or other important hospitality issues. After the final "The Lord be with you," the presider blesses the people in the name of God. Before 1570, priests blessed each individual with a simple sign of the cross because only popes and bishops were allowed to give formal blessings for entire congregations. Today, the formal blessing is the main action of the dismissal rite, and people strongly respond "Amen." Then, priests say "Go in peace to love and serve the world," and people respond "Thanks be to God." This final blessing is like saying good-bye, and it signifies Christianity going into daily action. After these dismissal words, some liturgical ministers begin to process while an ending hymn of praise is sung or appropriate instrumental music (or silence) takes place. After the procession reaches the back of church, all disperse. Presiders meet people individually as they exit. Some people hand out bulletins and church newspapers as others gather outside or in a parish hall for socializing and faith sharing. After people leave church, their mission is to "love and serve the world" by being Christian in daily life circumstances.

Prepare youngsters to fully participate in the dismissal rite and recessional by practicing responses, taking part in a procession, and providing opportunities for love and service within family, neighborhood, or school setting. First, the catechist, teacher, or parent can play the role of presider and direct students to answer the priest's greeting, blessing, and word of dismissal with "And also with you," "Amen," and "Thanks be to God." Remind youngsters that dismissal words send church members out to do good deeds for themselves, their families, and for other people, such as visiting the elderly or cheerfully helping their parents with house chores. Then guide children to process or walk through the congregation by taking parts of cross-bearer, lectionary carrier, servers and priest, just as these people had done for the entrance procession. Sing a familiar hymn of praise or play some instrumental music as students walk to the back of the church or room.

Ask children to suggest simple things they can do for others during the week and to choose one or two as a "mission" project—something youngsters send themselves to do just as their parents send them out to do errands. Activities can be simple for younger students; they can draw pictures for each member of their family. Older students can form a cleanup group to clear a trash-ridden lot for use as a park, playground, or a safe walking area. Let the activities fit the children's capabilities. Most children enjoy helping people or making others happy. However, participating in liturgical action and doing something good as a continuation of the eucharistic liturgy will make more meaningful the dismissal rite, recessional hymn, music or silence, and the chosen good action.

PART THREE

Experience as Preparation

17

Presence at Worship

One of the common religious expressions throughout various world cultures is the sharing of religious stories and the sacred, sacrificial meal. For Christians, eucharistic liturgy is the central expression of religious faith. Since the Last Supper, liturgical celebration has been the Catholic Church's official form of Sunday worship. By celebrating eucharistic liturgy, Christians remember Christ's paschal mystery within a community worship context.

Parents, teachers, catechists, priests, and liturgical ministers lead children to appreciate liturgy. In children's liturgies, adults need to balance structure and spontaneity to meet children's needs. When children are prepared to experience the rhythm of slowly spoken prayer, responses, readings, plus times of listening, silence, and bodily movement or song, youngsters feel secure; their positive behavior will show they expect to celebrate a religious event. Also, when students see their contributions gracefully incorporated into the liturgical celebration, strong interest will deepen participation because their work has been accepted and approved.

Following a planned format and making atmosphere ripe for children to pray demands alertness. Beginning on time and expressing liturgical theme intelligibly from liturgy's start is crucial. All liturgical materials should be ready and in position. Children, adults, presider, greeters, readers, servers, song leaders, musicians, and eucharistic ministers can reverently accomplish their individual roles in prescribed ways yet function as one Body of Christ praying Word and Eucharist. Distinct and deliberate enunciation of all sung and spoken liturgy sections allows liturgical celebration to be understood clearly. Everyone's actions and attitudes should obviously express and engage children and adults in prayer and be perfect, worthy, liturgical signs.

Adults do much to prepare children for liturgy. Helping youngsters to use all their senses enables them to experience liturgy. Then they begin to appreciate liturgical objects, ritual body language, liturgical dancing, and the benefits of good planning. Also, youngsters start to feel and understand the rhythm of sounds, silences, and religious music; they learn how to create their own worship environment.

During experiential and instructional sessions conducted by adults, children learn the parts of the eucharistic liturgy and the appropriate behavior that accompanies each segment. Soon, the children know how to gather themselves physically, psychologically, and spiritually before liturgical celebration and how to renew relationships through penitential or baptismal promise prayer forms. After a time, youngsters see the pattern of liturgy: gathering, entrance rite, Liturgy of the Word, transition from Word to Eucharist, Liturgy of the Eucharist, and the dismissal rite followed by recessional music. As youngsters experience this pattern through repeated demonstrations, paraliturgies, and eucharistic liturgy itself, they can participate more. This participation is possible when adults create opportunities for children to participate fully in liturgy.

A liturgy celebrated from the heart fosters unity with God and community. Clear, simple, reverent rite and ritual signs and symbols enable children to focus properly on liturgy. The Word proclaimed as well as heard and Eucharist shared in memory of Jesus is the experience of liturgy. Liturgical rite and ritual exist to convey that whole message. Then youngsters begin to pray to God as a person who cares for them. Also, they may feel a special sense of belonging and contribution to God's family. Most of all, children will remember Jesus in listening and hearing God's Word and in partaking of his Body and Blood.

18

Liturgy Is for Life: A Eucharistic Liturgy for Peace

In these days of heightened awareness of the need for nuclear freeze and disarmament, children may express the need to pray about this issue within the liturgical context. What follows is a suggested structure within which children may pray for peacemaking and take social action. Adult guidance is helpful for each segment of this peace liturgy.

Start with a scriptural background. In Micah 4:1-4, the Hebrew Bible Micah told his people that God's Kingdom would have good rules. This man said war materials would be made into farming tools. In Colossians 3:12-15, St. Paul asked his friends the Colossians to be kind and patient. He asked them to forgive and to love each other. In Matthew 5:1-12, Jesus taught his friends to be peacemakers for his sake. Adults aid children in applying these concepts to everyday experience. As we celebrate liturgy and live Christian lives, we try to follow good rules, to forgive, and to love each other. We hope to be peacemakers by saying "No" to weapons and war.

A typical lesson on peacemaking consists of learning to settle arguments by talking about problems, being fair and forgiving, plus protesting weapons-making.

1. Talking about problems. What does it mean? How do we do it? Does it really work?

2. Being fair and forgiving. How are we fair and forgiving? Why?

3. Protesting weapons-making. Why do we protest? What are different ways to do that? How can we protest? What is civil disobedience? Allow students to share experiences and ideas. Ask if any students have joined peace marches, demonstrations, rallies, actions or prayer services.

Two other peacemaking activities are:

1. Divide students into groups to make banners. Suggest some sayings or mottoes such as, "Say No

to War, Say Yes To Life"; "Talk and Forgive"; "Don't Fight"; "Bread Not Bombs"; "Peace to All People and All Living Things," etc.

2. Prepare readings and songs for liturgy by practicing them.

When celebrating liturgy, the presider may use prayers from "Mass for Peace and Justice" (Sacramentary, 902-903). Students and adults may sing whatever variation they know for liturgical celebration parts such as "Lord Have Mercy," "Alleluia," etc.

Students can process with their banners into the liturgy place. Then, they can place banners in pre-planned positions as the opening song is ended.

The following are appropriate entrance songs:

"Peace to You and Me" (*Hi God! 3*, Carey Landry)

"Neighbors" (*Hi God! 3*, Tom Colvin)

"Celebrate God" (*Hi God! 1, Carey Landry*)

"Prayer of St. Francis" (*Young Peoples Glory & Praise*, Sebastian Temple).

After the forgiveness rite, the following readings can be proclaimed:

1. Micah 4:1-4,2

2. Psalm 72:1-4,7-8,12-13,17 with the response: "May people be fair and live in peace."

3. Colossians 3: 12-15

4. Matthew 5: 1-12

Celebrants can read each Gospel section and relate it to banner messages and student experiences. You might want to sing: "We Come to Ask Forgiveness" (*Hi God!* 3, Carey Landry).

Students can be guided to formulate their own petitions for the prayer of the faithful. Possible offertory songs to use are "What Color Is God's Skin" (*Hi God!* 1, Carey Landry) or "What Shall I Do When I Hurt My Brother" (*Hi God!* 3, Carey Landry).

Music for the kiss of peace may include: "Peace Is Flowing Like A River," "Peace, My Friends," and "Peacetime" (all in *Hi God!* 1, Carey Landry).

Processional eucharistic hymns can be: "Communion Medley" (*Hi God!* 3) and "His Banner Over Me Is Love" (*Hi God!* 1), both by Carey Landry.

For the communion meditation, children can listen to or join in reciting the poem: "The Box" (*Poems, Prayers, and Promises,* John Denver) or the songs "Let There Be Peace On Earth" (*Young Peoples Glory & Praise,* Sy Miller and Jill Jackson), "Song of the Loving Father" (*Hi God!* 2, Carey Landry) and any appropriate popular songs on radio or TV that have similar messages.

Following the blessing, students may assemble with their banners and process behind the priest.

For the recessional, students can sing: "We Are the Light of the World" (*We Celebrate*, Jean Anthony Grief), "Come, Lord Jesus," "Friends Are Like Flowers" (*Hi God!* 2, Carey Landry) or the music of Joe Wise and Jack Miffleton.

Liturgy continues with the following social actions:

1. Join with your local Pax Christi group or church/neighborhood for prayer, study, or action against nuclear warfare and for peaceful solutions.

2. Read *Wacky and His Fuddlejig* by Stanford Summers, self-published, 484 W. 43rd St. #24-C, New York, NY, 10036 (against toy weapons production)

3. Send a stamped, self-addressed envelope to "It's Our World, Too!" P.O. Box 326, Winterport, ME, 04496. Ask for information on what students ages five to eighteen have come to work on against nuclear arms production and warfare.

4. Write to Friends General Conference, Interfaith Witness, Philadelphia Yearly Meeting, 1515 Cherry St., Philadelphia, PA, 19102. Send $5.00 for a Peace Packet of ideas.

5. Organize a peace vigil with adults. During the time together, sing peace songs from the following anthologies:

a. Bausch, Michael, and Ruth Duck. *Everflowing Streams*. NY: Pilgrim Press, 1981.

b. Religious Education Committee. *Songs of the Spirit*. Philadelphia, 1978. Write to Friends General Conference, Religious Education Committee, at above address.

APPENDIX A

The Liturgical Year

Many parishes have liturgical celebrations with both children and adults present for Sundays. However, churches, parish and regional schools, youth groups, or CCD classes may occasionally celebrate children's liturgy on weekdays. Although the idea of theme Masses is taboo for good Sunday liturgy, one idea or point for children's liturgy is pedagogically sound. On that note, the following is an idea list following the liturgical seasons of the year. Another good source of ideas is my book, *Seasonal Stories for Family Festivals* (Resource Publications, Inc., 1987).

Advent:
late November - most of December

1. Sunday or weekday scriptures

2. St. Nicholas, December 6

3. Immaculate Conception, December 8

4. Our Lady of Guadalupe, December 12

5. Gaudete (Joyful) Sunday

6. Posadas (Journey of Mary and Joseph), December 16-23

7. O Antiphons, December 17-23

8. Advent Calendars, December 1-24

Christmas Season:
December 25 - February 2

1. Christmas

2. Sunday or weekday scriptures

3. Mass for Peace, December 31

4. Mary, Mother of God, January 1

5. Holy Family Sunday

6. Epiphany, January 6

7. Baptism of the Lord

8. Water-into-Wine Sunday

9. Candlemas and Our Lady of the Candles, Puerto Rico, February 2

Ordinary Time:
February 3 - Ash Wednesday

1. Sunday or weekday scriptures

2. St. Blaise, February 3

3. St. Valentine, February 14

4. Heroes: Washington, Lincoln

5. Unsung heroes: Catholic Schools' Week

    a. Jesus, the teacher

    b. Moses, the teacher

    c. All South American teachers killed for their community leadership and the battle against illiteracy.

6. Carnivale (Sunday before Lent): eat meat before Lenten abstinence from meat (pre-Vatican II); the Lord of the Dance, Rejoicing in the face of death

7. Shrove Tuesday, Mardi Gras

Lent:
Ash Wednesday - Holy Saturday

1. Sunday or weekday scriptures
2. Laetare (Rose) Sunday (visit church where you were baptized)
3. St. Patrick's Day, March 17
4. Palm Sunday, The Passion Story
5. St. Joseph's Day, March 19
6. Passover, The Lord's Supper
7. Good Friday
8. Holy Saturday

Easter:
Easter Vigil - Pentecost Eve

1. Sunday or weekday scriptures
2. Renewal of baptismal vows
3. Blessing of Gardens, Easter Week, esp. Bright Friday
4. First Communion
5. Mother's Day

6. May Crowning

7. Ascension Thursday

8. Pentecost Eve

Pentecost Season or Ordinary Time

1. Sunday or weekday scriptures

2. Pentecost, Green Sunday (celebrate the Holy Spirit with green plant life)

3. Trinity Sunday (use Rublev's icon of the Trinity to decorate the shrine altar)

4. Corpus Christi Liturgy and Procession

5. Sacred Heart

6. Jesus Is Our Friend (end of ten-month schools)

7. Friendship Liturgy (end of ten-month schools)

8. St. John the Baptist Liturgy and Procession, June 24

9. St. Benedict, July 11

10. St. Mary Magdalen, July 22

11. Sts. Joachim and Ann, July 26

12. Lammas or Loaf Mass Sunday (Blessing first wheat crop)

13. St. Dominic, August 8

14. Transfiguration Sunday

15. Assumption of Mary, August 15

16. Labor Day (Blessing of Tools)

17. Welcome Back to School Mass
    (Celebrate Friends)

18. Holy Cross Sunday, mid-September

19. St. Michael, the Archangel,
    last week in September

20. Celebrate Life Sunday, first Sunday in October

21. The Guardian Angels, October 2

22. St. Francis, October 4

23. Anointing of sick and aged people,
    fourth Sunday of October

24. Halloween

25. All Saints Day

26. All Souls Day (Pray or chant a litany of the saints.)

27. St. Frances Xavier Cabrini, November 13

28. Thanksgiving

29. Christ the King

APPENDIX B

More Messages and Symbols to Use

The following are more messages and symbols to use during the children's Liturgy of the Word. Begin with the first part of the sentence, "Today, Jesus says to you, N...," and finish with the appropriate message, handing the child the accompanying symbol.

"Today, Jesus says to you, N....,"

Message: "Welcome others as I welcome you."

Symbol: nametag saying, "Hello! My name is _____."

Message: "Keep the commandments."

Symbol: Moses' tablets (made of paper), numbered I - X

Message: "Jesus loves you."

Symbol: A heart

Message: "I can see!" (Jesus healed man born blind.)

Symbol: Happy face with big eyes

Message: "Knock and the door will open."

Symbol: Door or keyhole

Message: "Help one another on the journey."

Symbol: Suitcase or knapsack

Message: "Don't be afraid, I am with you."

Symbol: Small boat on blue water

Message: "Blessed are you." (From the Beatitudes)

Symbol: Sign of the Cross

Use the following materials to make the symbols:

tiny household items
wrapping paper designs
index cards
bookmarks
seeds, stickers
rulers
pencils
valentine cut-outs
construction paper shapes
juice containers
sample pieces of fabric

Sources and Suggested Reading

Introduction

Bernardin, Joseph L. *Let the Children Come to Me.* Cincinnati: St. Anthony Messenger Press, 1976.

"Catechetics for Children." *Origins* 5, no. 47. (May 13, 1976): 746.

Faucher, W. Thomas, and Ione C. Nieland. *Touching God.* Notre Dame: Ave Maria Press, 1975.

Fleming, Austin. *Preparing for Liturgy: A Theology and Spirituality*. Washington, D.C.: The Pastoral Press, 1985.

Hovda, Robert W. *Strong, Loving and Wise: Presiding in Liturgy*. Collegeville, MN: The Liturgical Press, 1985.

Mitchell, Nathan. "The Once and Future Child: Towards a Theology of Childhood." *The Living Light* 12, no. 3 (Fall, 1975): 423-437.

Scheihing Cutler, Theresa, with Louis M. Savary. *Our Treasured Heritage-Teaching Christian Meditation to Children*. New York: Crossroad/Continuum, 1981.

Simons, George F. *Faces and Facets—A Workbook for the Liturgical Celebrant*. Cleveland, OH: Life In Christ, ACTA Foundation, 1977.

Chapter 1: Visual

Abbot, Walter M., S.J. "Constitution on the Sacred Liturgy." *The Documents of Vatican II*. New York: William H. Sadlier Inc., 1975.

Beirne, Steve and Kathy. *The Family Book of Scripture, Book 2*. Huntington, IN: Our Sunday Visitor, Inc., 1981.

Curley, Ed and Maureen. *First Prayers for Young Catholics.* Dayton, OH: Peter Li, Inc., 1984.

Ehlen, Margaret, I.H.M. *Remember—Liturgy Activity Book.* Beverly Hills, CA: Benziger, 1975.

Foley, Rita. *The Art of Teaching Religion.* New York: William H. Sadlier Inc., 1975.

Hynes, Arleen. *The Passover Meal.* Mahwah, NJ: Paulist Press, 1975.

Shanz, J.P. *The Sacraments and the Life of Worship.* Milwaukee: The Bruce Publishing Company, 1960.

Chapter 2: Tactile

Bishop's Committee on the Liturgy. *The Mystery of Faith.* Washington, DC: Federation of Diocesan Liturgical Commissions, 1981.

Brusselmans, Christiane, and Brian A. Haggerty. *We Celebrate the Eucharist—Guidelines for Parent and Catechist.* Morristown, NJ: Silver Burdett & Ginn, 1972.

Ehlen, Margaret, I.H.M. *Sign—Liturgy Activity Book.* Beverly Hills, CA: Benziger, 1975.

Fisherfolk. *God Is For Me: I'm Gonna Run, Run, Run.* Kansas City, MO: Credence Cassettes, 1980s. (Songbooks, cassettes)

McBride, Alfred A., O.Praem. Chapter 5 in *Creative Teaching in Christian Education.* Boston, MA: Allyn and Bacon, Inc., 1978.

Searle, Mark. *Liturgy Made Simple.* Collegeville, MN: The Liturgical Press, 1981.

Chapter 3: Kinesthetic

Daniels, Marilyn. *The Dance in Christianity: The History of Religious Dance Through the Ages.* Mahwah, NJ: Paulist Press, 1981.

DeSola, Carla. *The Spirit Moves: A Handbook of Dance and Prayer.* Washington, DC: Liturgical Conference, 1977.

Freed, Margaret De Haan. *A Time to Teach, A Time to Dance.* Sacramento, CA: Jalmar Press, Inc., 1976.

Foley, Edward. *Music In Ritual: A Pre-Theological Investigation.* Washington, DC: The Pastoral Press, 1985.

Gagne, Ronald, Thomas Kane, and Robert VerEecke. *Introducing Dance In Christian Worship.* Wash-ington, DC: The Pastoral Press, 1985.

Hollis, Sr. Mary Alverna, O.P. *Signs for Catholic Liturgy and Education.* Silver Springs, MD: The National Catholic Offices of the Deaf, 1981.

Lewis, Murshid Samuel L. *Sufi Dance and Song (Ecumenical),* vols. 1 and 2. San Francisco, CA: Sufi Islamia Ruhaniat Society, 1982. (Cassettes, song/dance book)

Murphy, Jack, and Arlene Wrigley. *Doing, Dance and Drama.* Notre Dame, IN: Ave Maria Press, 1980.

Riekehof, Lottie L. "Religious Signs." *The Joy of Signing.* Springfield, MO: The Gospel Publishing House, 1963.

DANCERS

DeSola, Carla. St. John the Divine Cathedral, New York, NY.

Fredgren, Katherine. Washington, DC and Alexan-dria, Virginia: Protestant and Episcopal Churches.

Gallaudet Dance Troupe. Gallaudet College, 7th
and Florida, N.E., Washington, DC, 20012

Weyman, Gloria

Chapter 4: Smelling and Tasting

Hildegard of Bingen. "The Six Days of Creation
Re-newed." *Illuminations of Hildegard of
Bingen.* Santa Fe, New Mexico: Bear and
Company, 1985.

Gy, P. M. "The Idea of Christian Initiation." *Studia
Liturgica* 12. (1977):174-5.

Mackintosh, Sam. *Passover Seder for Christian
Families.* San Jose, California: Resource
Publications, Inc., 1984.

Rabelais, Maria. *Children Celebrate!* Mahwah, New
Jersey: Paulist Press, 1975.

Schmemann, Alexander. *Liturgy and Life:
Christian Development Through Liturgical
Experience.* Syosset, New York: Orthodox
Church in America, 1974.

Tarasar, Constance. Diane Apostolos, ed. "Taste
and See." *The Sacred Play of Children.* New
York: Seabury Press, 1983.

Chapter 5: Structure

Collins, John P. *These Forty Days—A Lenten Journey for Young People and Their Parents.* Piermont-on-the-Hudson, New York: Catholic Heritage Press, 1980.

Collins, Mary. "Liturgical Methodology and the Cultural Evolution of Worship in the United States." *Worship* 49, no. 2. (February, 1975):85-102.

Eliade, Mircea. *Rites and Symbols of Initiation.* New York: Harper & Row, Publishers Inc., 1975.

Gamm, Rev. David B. *Child's Play.* Notre Dame, IN: Ave Maria Press, 1978. (Scripture-based plays for grades three to eight)

Olivier, John H., S.S. "Of Parties and Sunday Worship." *Modern Liturgy* 9, no. 4. (June/July, 1982):8.

Schroeder, Ted, Linda, Christopher, Joel, and Mark. *Celebrate While We Wait.* St. Louis, MO: Concordia Publishing House, 1977. (Christmas, Advent activities)

Searle, Mark, ed. *Parish: A Place for Worship.* Collegeville, MN: The Liturgical Press, 1981.

Smith, Gregory. "Show One Another a Good Time." *Living Worship* 15, no. 7. (August/September, 1979).

Villot, Jean Card. "Directory for Masses with Chil-dren." *The Sacramentary*. Huntington, NY: Our Sunday Visitor, 1974.

Walsh, Eugene A., S.S. *The Theology of Celebration*. Old Hickory, TN: Pastoral Arts Associates of North America, 1977.

CASSETTES

Duffy, Regis. *The Symbolizing Community*. Kansas City, MO: Credence Cassettes, 1980s. (5 hrs., 30 mins.)

Gallen, John. *Liturgical Spirituality*. Kansas City, MO: Credence Cassettes, 1980s. (4 hrs., 30 mins.)

Guzie, Tad. *They Gathered for the Breaking of the Bread*. Kansas City, MO: Credence Cassettes, 1980s. (51 mins.)

Searle, Mark. *Basic Liturgy*. Kansas City, MO: Credence Cassettes, 1980s. (4 hrs.)

Walsh, Eugene, S.S. *The Community's Guide to Sunday Mass*. Kansas City, MO: Credence Cassettes, 1980s. (3 hrs., 30 mins.)

Chapter 6: Sounds and Silences

Bernier, Paul, S.S.S. *Bread Broken and Shared*. Notre Dame, IN: Ave Maria Press, 1981.

Dooley, Kate. *Celebrate God's Mighty Deeds*. Mahwah, NJ: Paulist Press, 1972.

Fox, Matthew. *On Becoming a Musical Mystical Bear*. Mahwah, NJ: Paulist Press, 1976.

Huck, Gabe. *Liturgy Needs Community Needs Liturgy*. Mahwah, NJ: Paulist Press, 1981.

Hultstrand, Donald M. *The Praying Church*. New York: Seabury Press, 1977.

Otto, Rudolf. *The Idea of the Holy*. New York: Oxford University Press, 1923.

Peterfly, Sr. Ida, et al. *Prayer—God Speaks and Listens*. Kansas City, MO: Credence Cassettes, 1988. (Script, 30 min. video)

Searle, Mark. *Sunday Morning: A Time for Worship*. Collegeville, MN: The Liturgical Press, 1982.

Chapter 7: Auditory

Bishop's Committee on the Liturgy. *Music in Catholic Worship*. Washington, DC: National Catholic Worship Conference, 1972.

Brown, Judith Gwyn. *I Sing a Song of the Saints of God*. Somers, CT: Seabury Press, 1981.

Coates, Paul, and Timothy Crowley. *All God's People Love To Sing—Teacher's Guidebook*. Phoenix, AZ: North American Liturgy Resources, 1984.

Jasper, Tony, ed. *The Illustrated Family Hymn Book*. Somers, CT: Seabury Press, 1981.

Landry, Carey. *Hi God!* 2. Phoenix, AZ: North American Liturgy Resources, 1976.

Peterfly, Sr. Ida., et al. *Spiral Songbook (with tapes)*. Kansas City, MO: Credence Cassettes, 1988.

White, Jack Noble. *Everything You Need for Children's Worship—Except Children*. Cincinnati, OH: St. Anthony Messenger Press, 1981.

CASSETTES, RECORDS, VIDEOS

Fisherfolk. *Leading Worship with the Guitar.*
Kansas City, MO: Credence Cassettes, 1980s.
(VHS, 28 mins.)

He Shall Be Peace. *The Seed: Solitude.* Old
Hickory, TN: Pastoral Arts Associates of North
America, 1980s.

Landry, Carey, and Carol Jean Kinghorn. *Hi God!*
2, 3; *Psalms for Children: Color the World.*
Phoenix, AZ: North American Liturgy Resources,
1970s, 1980s.

Louvat, Lorraine. *I Could Have Been A Bumblebee;*
Love Is A Magic Feeling. Dubuque, IA: Wm. C.
Brown Company Publishers, 1980s.

Maranatha Music. *Psalms Alive.* Costa Mesa, CA:
Word, Inc., 1980s.

Miffleton, Jack. *Promise Chain—Songs of Hope*
and Self-Discovery for Children. Chicago, IL:
World Library Publications, Inc., 1979.

Miller, Rev. Jim, Bob Smith, and Tim Valentine. *In*
Our God. Phoenix, AZ: North American Liturgy
Resources, 1984.

Okun, Milton, and Phil Perkins, eds. *Bullfrogs and Butterflies*. Canoga Park, CA: Sparrow-Birdwing Music, 1978.

Pinson, Joe. *Popular Collection of Sacred Music for Children*. Phoenix, AZ: North American Liturgy Resources, 1980s.

Shaw, Jim, and Kathy Kanavy. *Gift of Song*. Huntington, IN: Our Sunday Visitor, Inc., 1982.

Walker, Mary Lu, Jim Shaw, and Rosemary Stoffel. *Celebrating Songs*. Huntington, IN: Our Sunday Visitor, Inc., 1982.

Walker, Mary Lu. *Dandelions, Peaceable Kingdom, and Songs for Your Children*. Trumansberg, NY: K & R Music, Inc., 1970s, '80s.

Wise, Joe. *Close Your Eyes, Show Me Your Smile and Welcome In*. Old Hickory, TN: Pastoral Arts Associates, 1970s, '80s.

Chapter 8: Atmosphere

Blandford, Sr. Elizabeth, S.C.N., and Sr. Janet Marie Bucher, C.D.P. *Come Out!—Celebrations for Children, Ages 2 to 8*. Chicago, IL: World Library Publications, Inc., 1971.

Heyer, George. *Signs of Our Times: Theological Essays on Art in the Twentieth Century.* Grand Rapids, MI: Wm. B. Eerdmans Publishing Co., 1980.

O'Day, Rey, and Edward Powers. *Theatre of the Spirit.* New York: The Pilgrim Press, 1981.

Ortegel, Sr. Adelaide. *Banners and Such.* San Jose, CA: Resource Publications, Inc., 1981.

Snyder, Bernadette McCaver. *Hoorays and Hosannas.* Notre Dame, IN: Ave Maria Press, 1970s.

United States Catholic Conference. *Environment and Art in Catholic Worship.* Washington, D.C.: United States Catholic Conference, 1978.

Vosko, Richard S. *Through the Eye of a Rose Window.* San Jose, CA: Resource Publications, Inc., 1981.

Wolterstorff, Nicholas. *Art in Action: Towards a Christian Aesthetic.* Grand Rapids, MI: Wm. B. Eerdmans Publishing Co., 1980.

VIDEO

Cronin, Jim and Gaynell. *Effective Teaching Methods* 1, Mahwah, NJ: Paulist Press, 1988. (60 mins., includes study guide)

Chapter 9: Gathering

Brusselmans, Christiane, with Edward Watkin. *Religion For Little Children*. Huntington, IN: Our Sunday Visitor, Inc., 1970.

Farrell, Rev. Edward J., S.T.L. *Celtic Meditations*. Denville, NJ: Dimensions Books, Inc., 1976.

Holmes, Urban T. "Parents and Children in Prayer." *Liturgy*. (April 1974).

Hurley, Karen, ed. *Why Sunday Mass?* Cincinnati, OH: St. Anthony Messenger Press, 1972.

Jones, Alexander, ed. "St. Luke" and "The Acts of the Apostles." *The Jerusalem Bible*. Garden City, NY: Doubleday and Company, Inc., 1966.

Kinghorn, Carol Jean, and Carey Landry. *Celebrating Jesus*. Phoenix, AZ: North American Liturgy Resources, 1977.

Ryan, Mary Perkins. "Children Grow, Parents Grow, Church Grows." *New Catholic World* (March/April 1973):216, 84-88.

Chapter 10: Reconciliation and Renewal

Emminghaus, Johannes H. *The Eucharist: Essence, Form, Celebration.* Collegeville, MN: The Liturgical Press, 1978.

Hellwig, Monika. *The Sacrament of Penance Today.* Collegeville, MN: The Liturgical Press, 1985. (Script, 2 filmstrips, 2 cassettes)

Jungmann, Josef. *The Mass.* Collegeville, MN: The Liturgical Press, 1975.

Patino, J., ed. *The New Order of Mass.* Collegeville, MN: The Liturgical Press, 1970.

Peterfly, Sr. Ida, et al. *Forgiveness—the Loving Touch of God.* Kansas City, MO: Credence Cassettes, 1985. (Script, 30 min. video)

Thiry, Joan. *Sharing His Love—Celebrating First Confession.* Dayton, OH: Peter Li, Inc., 1981.

Roguet, A.M. *The New Mass.* New York, NY: Catholic Book Publishing Co., 1970.

Walsh, Eugene, A., S.S. *Gathering For Each Other*.
Old Hickory, TN: Pastoral Arts Associates of
North America, 1981.

Chapter 11: Entrance

Bishops' Committee on the Liturgy. *The Mystery of
Faith*. Washington, DC: Federation of Diocesan
Liturgical Commissions, 1981.

Collins, Rev. Patrick. *Understanding the Mass*.
Mahwah, NJ: Paulist Press, 1988. (Script, 55
min. cassette)

Gelineau, J., S.J. "Music and Singing in the
Liturgy." *The Study of Liturgy*. New York:
Oxford University Press, 1978.

Howell, Clifford, S.J. *Mean What You Say*.
Collegeville, MN: The Liturgical Press, 1965.

Scheemann, Alexander. *Liturgy and Life: Christian
Development through Liturgical Experience*.
New York: Department of Religious Education,
Orthodox Church in America, 1974.

Walsh, Eugene A., S.S. *The Order of Mass:
Guidelines*. Old Hickory, TN: Pastoral Arts
Associates of North America, 1979.

Chapter 12: The Word

Emminghaus, Johannes H. *The Eucharist: Essence, Form, Celebration*. Collegeville, MN: The Liturgical Press, 1978.

Huck, Gabe. *Liturgy With Style and Grace*. Chicago, IL: Liturgy Training Program, 1978.

Jungmann, Josef, S.J. *The Liturgy of the Word*. Collegeville, MN: The Liturgical Press, 1966.

Sloyan, Gerard, S. *Liturgy in Focus*. Mahwah, NJ: Paulist Press, 1964.

Twenty-sixth North American Liturgical Week. *Jesus Christ Reforms His Church*. Washington, DC: The Liturgical Conference, 1966.

Scheihing Cutler, Theresa. *Meditations for Children* and *Meditations for Families*. Kansas City, MO: Credence Cassettes, 1981.

Scheihing Cutler, Theresa, with Louis Savary. *Our Treasured Heritage—Teaching Christian Meditation for Children*. New York: Crossroad/Continuum, 1981.

Chapter 13: The Word with Children

Apostolos-Cappadona, Diane, ed. *The Sacred Play of Children.* New York: The Seabury Press, 1983.

Berglund, Mary Catherine. *Gather the Children (Cycle B).* Washington, DC: The Pastoral Press.

Cronin, Gaynell. *Sunday Throughout the Week.* Notre Dame, IN: Ave Maria Press, 1981.

Ihli, Sr. Jan. *Liturgy of the Word for Children.* Mahwah, NJ: Paulist Press, 1979.

Weekday Lectionary for Masses with Children. Collegeville, MN: The Liturgical Press, 1985.

VIDEOS AND TAPES

Brusselmans, Christiane. *Children's Liturgies.* Waldwick, NJ: Arena Lettres, 1977.

Cronin, Gaynell. *Effective Teaching Methods* 2. Mahwah, NJ: Paulist Press, 1988. (60 mins.)

Pfeifer, Carl, and Janaan Manternach. *Understanding the Mass for Children. Mahwah, NJ: Paulist Press, 1988. (40 mins.)*

The Liturgical Press. *The World God Made/Noah's Ark* (30 min.); *The Little Boat That Almost*

Sank/The Man Who Couldn't Wait (20 min.);
The Princess and the Baby/The Great Escape
(20 min.) Collegeville, MN: The Liturgical Press,
1985.

Veritas. *Reading in Church.* Kansas City, MO:
Credence Cassettes, 1988. (61 mins.)

Chapter 14:
Transition from Word to Eucharist

Abbott, Walter, S.J., Ed. "Constitution on the
Sacred Liturgy." *The Documents of Vatican II.*
New York: The America Press, 1966.

Bishops' Committee on the Liturgy. *The Mystery of
Faith.* Washington, DC: Federation of Diocesan
Liturgical Commissions, 1980.

Crichton, J. D. *The Mass and the People of God.*
Collegeville, MN: The Liturgical Press, 1966.

Patino, J., ed. *The New Order of Mass.* Collegeville,
MN: The Liturgical Press, 1970.

Walsh, Eugene A., S.S. *The Order of Mass:
Guidelines.* Old Hickory, TN: Pastoral Arts
Associates of North America, 1979.

Chapter 15: The Eucharist

Bishops' Committee on the Liturgy. *Eucharistic Prayers for Masses with Children and for Masses of Reconciliation.* Washington, DC: National Conference of Catholic Bishops, 1975.

Deiss, Lucien, C.S.Sp. *Springtime of the Liturgy.* Collegeville, MN: The Liturgical Press, 1979.

Gelineau, Joseph. *The Eucharistic Prayer: Praise of the Whole Assembly.* Washington, D.C.: The Pastoral Press, 1985.

Hamman, A., O.F.M. *The Paschal Mystery.* Montreal, Canada: Palm Publishers, 1970s

Jungmann, Josef A. *The Eucharistic Prayer.* Chicago, IL: Fides Publishers Association, 1956.

Kavanaugh, Rev. Aidan. "Through Him, With Him, and In Him." *U.S.Catholic.* (August, 1976).

Martimort, A.G., ed. *The Eucharist.* Collegeville, MN: The Liturgical Press, 1986.

Peterfly, Sr. Ida, et al. *Eucharist—Celebrating Union with Jesus and Each Other.* Kansas City, MO: Credence Cassettes, 1985. (Script, 30 min. video)

Soubigou, Louis. *A Commentary on the Prefaces and the Eucharistic Prayers of the Roman Missal.* Collegeville, MN: The Liturgical Press, 1971.

Chapter 16: Dismissal and Recession

Emminghaus, Johannes H. *The Eucharist.* Collegeville, MN: The Liturgical Press, 1978.

Hellwig, Monika K. *The Eucharist and the Hunger of the World.* Mahwah, NJ: Paulist Press, 1976.

Howell, Clifford, S.J. *Mean What You Say.* Collegeville, MN: The Liturgical Press, 1965.

Liturgy Training Program. *Liturgy With Style and Grace.* Chicago, IL: Archdiocese of Chicago, 1978.

Patino, J., ed. *The New Order of Mass.* Collegeville, MN: The Liturgical Press, 1970.

Richstatter, Thomas, O.F.M. "How to Participate More Actively in the Mass." *Catholic Update.* Cincinnati, OH: St. Anthony Messenger Press (August, 1982).

Chapter 17: Presence at Worship

Braso, Gabriel M., O.S.B. *Liturgy and Spirituality*.
Collegeville, MN: The Liturgical Press, 1971.

Bruck, Maria, ed. *More Children's Liturgies*.
Mahwah, NJ: Paulist Press, 1985.

Eliade, Mircea. *The Sacred and the Profane*. New
York: Harper & Row, Publishers Inc., 1959.

Egan, John. *Liturgy and Justice: An Unfinished
Agenda*. Collegeville, MN: The Liturgical Press,
1985.

Farrell, Edward. *The Prayer that Inspires Action
for Justice*. Kansas City, MO: Credence
Cassettes, 1980s. (Three cassettes, 2 hrs.)

Fox, Matthew. *A Spirituality Named Compassion*.
San Francisco, CA: Harper & Row, Publishers,
Inc., 1979.

Jungmann, Josef A. *The Mass*. Collegeville, MN:
The Liturgical Press, 1976.

Keifer, Ralph A. *Mass in Time of Doubt: The
Meaning of Mass for Catholics Today*.
Washington, DC: The Pastoral Press, 1984.

Kenny, R., S.H.M. *Children's Liturgies*. Mahwah, NJ: Paulist Press, 1970s.

Kinghorn, Carol Jean, and Carey Landry. *Celebrating Jesus*. Phoenix, AZ: North American Liturgy Resources, 1977.

Patino, J., ed. *The New Order of Mass*. Collegeville, MN: The Liturgical Press, 1970.

Searle, Mark. *Liturgy and Social Justice*. Collegeville, MN: The Liturgical Press, 1985.

Sobrino, Jon, S.J. Matthew Fox, ed. "Christian Prayer and New Testament Theology: A Basis for Social Justice and Spirituality." *Western Spirituality: Historical Roots, Ecumenical Routes*. Santa Fe, NM: Bear & Company, Inc., 1981.

Walsh, Eugene A., S.S. *The Theology of Celebration*; *The Ministry of the Celebrating Community*; and *Practical Suggestions for Celebrating Sunday Mass*. Old Hickory, TN: Pastoral Arts Associates of North America, 1977, 1977, and 1978 respectively.

Chapter 17: Liturgy Is for Life

Cloud, Kate, Ellie Deegan, Alice Evans, Hayat Imam, and Barbara Signer. *Watermelons Not War!* Philadelphia, PA: New Society Publishers, 1985.